BANGKOK

LOCAL

BANGKOK

CULT RECIPES FROM THE STREE

LOCAL

**SAREEN ROJANAMETIN &
JEAN THAMTHANAKORN**

FOOD PHOTOGRAPHY BY ALANA DIMOU

S THAT MAKE THE CITY

Smith
Street
Books

EARLY
12

MID
52

Introduction

Strolling through narrow alleyways with a piece of green mango in one hand and a tub of salt and chilli dip in the other, we found ourselves in Jatujak, the biggest weekend market in Bangkok. Considered one of the best markets the city has to offer, Jatujak is a favourite for tourists and locals alike. You can find anything here, from clothes, vintage treasures and traditional crafts to delicious street food and drinks. Across the road from Jatujak is one of the world's most famous fresh-food markets, Aor Tor Kor, where you can find produce from local farmers as well as street-food vendors from all over Thailand, cooking and serving their regional specialties.

These two markets perfectly encapsulate the significance of food and eating in Thai culture. Taking in the size, activity and the variety of sights and smells, you immediately gain an appreciation for how seriously culinary life is taken in Bangkok. Even daily conversation reflects the importance of food and eating to the Thai people: it's more common for locals to greet each other with 'Have you eaten yet?' than simply asking how someone is. Cooking isn't just done behind closed doors, in the kitchens of houses and restaurants; much of the best Thai food is cooked, served and eaten on the streets – celebrated out in the open.

The history of Thailand and its culinary culture dates back as far as the sixth century, when the Mon people began to migrate to the land, followed later by the Khmer, Malay and Tai peoples. By the fourteenth century the country was known to outsiders as Siam, and the

PAPAYA

capital of Siam's most powerful kingdom, the Ayutthaya Kingdom, was considered one of the most prosperous cities in the world, thanks to flourishing international trade and an influx of immigration.

During the Ayutthaya era (1351–1767), the Thai populace was exposed to new products, ways of living and, importantly, food. Various ingredients and dishes now thought of as Thai were originally brought to Siam by foreigners. Chilli was introduced by the Portuguese in the sixteenth century; many of the spices in Thai curries arrived with Indian merchants; and stir-frying over high heat was a method of cooking introduced by the Chinese. This rich history of foreign trade and cultural influence has contributed to the flavour profile and diversity of the Thai cuisine we know and love today.

Thailand's differing climates and landscapes affect the kinds of produce and resources available for cooking, and each region has its own traditions, dialects, cooking styles and signature dishes. These all collide in Thailand's capital, Bangkok, a city that is a melting pot of cultures, religions, people and cuisines – and a lively contrast to its more sedate countryside neighbours. For this reason, Bangkok has enticed millions of people from all around Thailand, who in turn weave their own ways of living and cooking into the city.

Bangkok is vast, brimming with areas both historic and new that sprawl outwards from the city centre. One of the oldest landmarks is Yaowarat, or Chinatown, which has been the heart of

the Thai–Chinese community since 1782. It's easy to spend all day here, exploring the streets and markets until the sky is dark and the city is bright with the lights and flames of street-food stalls offering everything from seafood and congee to offal soup and birds' nests in sugar syrup. One of the largest Chinatowns in the world, you would be forgiven for forgetting you're in Bangkok and not Hong Kong or Beijing.

Not too far away from Yaowarat is Ratchadamnoen Avenue, which passes through Rattanakosin, Bangkok's old city – home to the Grand Palace and the breathtaking Temple of the Emerald Buddha, along with other historically and culturally significant landmarks. Between Yaowarat and Ratchadamnoen Avenue there are street-food stalls on almost every corner, including the legendary Thipsamai Pad Thai, the oldest and one of the most popular pad thai vendors in the country.

On the other side of town is Sukhumvit Road, Thailand's longest road, which stretches from Bangkok to the city of Trat, more than 300 kilometres (186 miles)

COCONUT

away. In Bangkok, Sukhumvit Road is a major tourist and commercial district full of cafés, bars and shopping destinations, but quite light on more authentically Thai experiences. It is, however, the place to go for international cuisine, with a number of high-end restaurants featuring Italian, French, Japanese and American food, among others.

In contrast, Bangkok is also home to a number of floating markets, which allow you to experience how the locals of the past once lived: wooden houses alongside narrow canals, long-tail boats selling traditional Thai food and rare ancient desserts, and travelling via waterways, rather than roads.

Regardless of where you are in Bangkok, there will always be dedicated cooks and chefs hard at work in restaurants, on the streets and at markets, serving up authentic food to equally dedicated diners. Food is truly the heart of this city and its people, and both Bangkok and Thai cuisine never cease to surprise us. So join us in exploring the stories and recipes of this wonderful city, discovering new delights in your kitchen and at your dining table.

Chefs' notes

A mortar and pestle is the most important piece of equipment for cooking authentic Thai cuisine. It is used for preparing ingredients, such as relishes, curry pastes and spices, and the bigger your mortar and pestle, the easier it is to work with. We recommend you have one in your kitchen before trying the recipes in this book.

Rice is a staple for the Thai people and no matter how delicious the dishes are, a meal would not be complete without it. In this book we use jasmine rice, unless otherwise specified.

Gapi, or shrimp paste, is an essential ingredient in Thai cooking. Gapi is made from fermented shrimp, although Thai cooks do not usually make their own gapi as the fermentation process is a long one and the finished product is widely available in markets. Gapi is used in various curry pastes, stir-fries and soups, and it is the foundation of the much-loved shrimp paste relish nam prik gapi, which the locals usually serve alongside short mackerel and vegetables. Outside of Thailand, gapi can generally be purchased from Asian supermarkets.

The most widely used sugars in Thailand are palm sugar and coconut sugar. Some of the recipes in this book, especially the dessert recipes, specifically call for these. Palm sugar and coconut sugar must be finely sliced, grated or melted before mixing them with other ingredients. If a recipe calls for melted palm or coconut sugar, all you need to do is warm the quantity of sugar required in a saucepan over low heat until it liquefies.

Both coconut milk and coconut cream are used in Thai cooking, and it is important to know the difference between the two. Coconut milk has a thin consistency closer to cow's milk, whereas coconut cream is much thicker and richer. They both affect the flavour and texture of dishes differently and generally can't be substituted for one another. Some recipes in this book, especially curry recipes, call for you to 'crack' coconut cream; this refers to frying coconut cream until the oil separates from the other coconut solids. This is usually then combined with a curry paste, resulting in a more concentrated, flavourful curry.

Nam prik pao, or Thai chilli paste, is another common ingredient in Thai cuisine. Originating in central Thailand, it is made from dried chillies, red shallots and garlic. Thais rarely make chilli paste themselves as it is widely available at local markets. Outside of Thailand, nam prik pao can be found in Asian supermarkets.

Nahm poon sai, or limewater, is another traditional ingredient, particularly in Thai desserts. It is an alkaline solution made by mixing slaked lime (calcium hydroxide) with water and, sometimes, turmeric powder. Nahm poon sai makes batters and pastries crisp and keeps fruit firm even after long cooking periods. The slaked lime needed to make nahm poon sai can be found in Thai supermarkets, and instructions for mixing your own limewater can be found on page 190.

The recipes in this book should be treated as a guide, not as hard and fast rules. In Thailand, it's customary for every home and every kitchen – every grandmother and mother – to have their own spin on a dish, adding a little here and there, experimenting, adjusting to their own tastes and cooking by instinct. It's why Thai cuisine is so beautiful, unique and diverse.

If you follow our recipes to the letter, the food will be delicious, of course, but if you prefer a dish a little sweeter, spicier, saltier or more sour – or wish to substitute an ingredient or two – go ahead and make the change. Creating these dishes won't be quite as much fun if you don't!

The very essence of Thai cuisine is in making the food your own. So read our recipes, try them out, then forget them and cook with your instincts. Keep tasting and adjusting again and again, and ultimately the food will truly be yours, not ours. Enjoy!

EA

RLY

EARLY

Mornings in Bangkok provide a beautiful insight into the Thai way of life and the vital role that food plays in Thai culture. At dawn, the city's inhabitants begin their morning routines with the preparation and donation of food to Buddhist monks, who leave their temples to accept these alms as part of their daily practice. Because the monks subsist solely on food offerings, giving to the monks is considered one of the ways to build good karma.

Sunrise sees street-food vendors setting up their stalls all over the city, cooking up various breakfast dishes for busy diners. Sitting down for a big breakfast is not the norm in Thailand, as the heavy traffic jams of the morning rush hour make it challenging to get anywhere on time. Instead, breakfast is usually something fast and easy: popular takeaway options include grilled pork skewers and glutinous rice, or soy milk and Chinese doughnuts. It's also not uncommon for rice, noodles and even curries to be eaten for breakfast, with many food stalls around the city offering such specialties from early in the morning.

Generally speaking, Thai people don't drink coffee on a regular basis, so cafés aren't as prevalent as they are in the West. Most coffee shops in Bangkok are overseas chain stores, but this has changed in recent times, with young locals opening up hip cafés serving espresso, filter coffee and pastries.

On weekends, the 'fast and easy' rule goes out the window. Morning meals at home may include steamed egg custard studded with prawns (shrimp), or rice soup with pork meatballs and condiments. Young people visit cafés for brunch, enjoying more Western-influenced breakfasts and beverages. Local markets are filled with shoppers, ready to cook for their families.

Our childhood memories of early weekend mornings in Bangkok are of visiting Lumpini Park. The park, a peaceful oasis situated in the midst of the city chaos, is well known for its beautiful greenery and its aerobic and tai chi practitioners, not to mention the street-food stalls serving up warm congee, Chinese-style buns and dim sum.

KHAI KRATA

Pan eggs

As the name might suggest, this simple breakfast dish is served in the small frying pan it's cooked in. Khai krata is similar to the weekend fry-ups you might already enjoy, and some believe the dish was influenced by Western breakfasts. Traditionally served with minced (ground) pork and Thai-style pork sausage, it's a meal that has become difficult to find in recent years. There are a few coffee houses in Bangkok's Old City that still serve khai krata with toast and Thai coffee, and they are definitely worth seeking out when you visit.

Serves 2

1 Chinese sausage (lap cheong), cut into 5 mm (¼ in) slices

1 pork sausage, such as chorizo

2 tablespoons grapeseed oil

1 tablespoon unsalted cultured butter

4 eggs

2 slices of ham

1 spring onion (scallion), finely sliced

freshly ground white pepper, to taste

Minced pork

2 tablespoons grapeseed oil

½ onion, finely diced

100 g (3½ oz) minced (ground) pork

4 banana prawns (shrimp), peeled and coarsely chopped

1 tablespoon oyster sauce

1 tablespoon soy sauce

freshly ground white pepper, to taste

1 First, prepare the minced pork. Heat the oil in a non-stick frying pan over medium heat. Stir-fry the onion until translucent, then add the minced pork and prawn. Increase the heat to high and cook, stirring constantly, for 2–3 minutes, until caramelised. Add the remaining minced pork ingredients and taste, adjusting the seasoning if necessary. Remove from the heat and set aside.

2 Bring a small saucepan of water to the boil over high heat. Add the sliced Chinese sausage and the whole pork sausage and boil for 5 minutes, then drain and pat dry with paper towel. Cut the pork sausage into 5 mm (¼ in) slices, if desired. Heat the oil in a non-stick frying pan over medium heat and pan-fry the sausages until caramelised on both sides. Remove from the heat and set aside.

3 Divide the butter between two small frying pans suitable for serving. Place the frying pans over medium heat and melt the butter, then add 2 eggs to each pan. Cover the pans and cook the eggs for 2 minutes. Uncover the pans and add the minced pork, sausages and ham, pressing them into the egg whites. Cover and cook the eggs, checking frequently, until they are done to your liking. Remove from the heat, sprinkle with spring onion and white pepper to taste.

4 Serve the khai krata in the pans they were cooked in, but be careful – the metal will still be hot.

Kahree Puff Gai

Chicken curry puffs

This seashell-like pastry is a favourite among Thailand's Muslim communities. Influenced by Portuguese desserts introduced to Thailand in the fourteenth century, it is a mixture of Western pastry and Eastern spices. Kahree puff can be filled with various ingredients, both savoury and sweet, with chicken being the most popular. They can be found in markets all over Bangkok, but the most popular destination for this dish is Saraburee, a province northeast of the city.

Makes 15

150 g (5½ oz) sweet potato, diced

2 tablespoons unsalted butter

50 g (1¾ oz) onion, diced

10 g (⅓ oz) red shallot, diced

100 g (3½ oz) chicken breast, diced

2 tablespoons soy sauce

15 g (½ oz) caster (superfine) sugar

1 tablespoon fine sea salt

½ tablespoon freshly ground white pepper

1 tablespoon curry powder

vegetable oil, for deep-frying

Inner puff pastry

70 g (2½ oz) plain (all-purpose) flour, plus extra for dusting

3 tablespoons grapeseed oil

Outer puff pastry

3 tablespoons Limewater (page 190)

3 tablespoons iced water

½ tablespoon caster (superfine) sugar

1 teaspoon fine sea salt

140 g (5 oz) plain (all-purpose) flour

3 tablespoons grapeseed oil

1 Fill a large bowl with iced water. Bring a saucepan of water to the boil over high heat and par-cook the sweet potato for 3–5 minutes, until slightly tender but not mushy or soft. Drain the sweet potato, then transfer to the iced water to refresh. Once cool, drain again and set aside.

2 Heat the butter in a non-stick frying pan over medium heat and stir-fry the onion until translucent, then add the shallot and cook until fragrant. Stir in the chicken breast, soy sauce, caster sugar, salt, white pepper and curry powder. Add the sweet potato and stir-fry until the mixture is well combined and dry. Remove from the heat and allow to cool to room temperature.

3 Meanwhile, make the inner puff pastry. Sift the flour through a mesh sieve into a mixing bowl. Make a well in the centre of the flour and pour in the oil. Use a spatula to gradually incorporate the flour until a dough is formed. Using your hands, knead until the dough is smooth. Set aside to rest for 10 minutes.

4 To make the outer puff pastry, combine the limewater, iced water, sugar and salt in a small bowl. Sift the flour through a mesh sieve into a mixing bowl. Make a well in the centre of the flour and pour in the oil and the limewater mixture. Use a spatula to gradually incorporate the flour until a dough is formed. Using your hands, knead until the dough just comes together. Set aside to rest for 10 minutes.

5 Divide the inner puff pastry dough into five equal balls weighing roughly 30 g (1 oz) each. Divide the outer puff pastry dough into five equal balls weighing 50 g (1¾ oz) each.

6 To assemble the puff pastry, lightly dust your work surface with flour and roll the outer puff pastry balls into discs just large enough to wrap around the inner puff pastry balls. Place an inner puff pastry ball in the centre of each outer puff pastry disc and wrap the outer discs around the inner balls to form five larger dough balls. Cover with a damp kitchen towel.

7 Lightly dust your work surface again. Place one dough ball seam-side down on the work surface and roll it out in one direction only until you have a rectangle 12–15 cm (4¾–6 in) long. Starting from the short edge closest to you, tightly roll the rectangle into a sausage. Rotate the sausage 90 degrees, so the short edge is close to you once again, then roll it out in one direction only until you have a rectangle 18–20 cm (7–7¾ in) long. Starting from the short edge closest to you, tightly roll the rectangle into a sausage once more and cut crossways into thirds. Place the thirds cut-side down on the work surface and roll out into ovals 2–3 mm (¹⁄₁₆–⅛ in) thick. Set aside, cover with a damp kitchen towel and repeat the process with the remaining dough balls.

8 To assemble the curry puffs, take one of the pastry ovals and place it on your palm. One side should have a more distinct spiral pattern on it; make sure the spiral side of the pastry is facing down. Place 1 tablespoon of filling in the centre of the pastry and brush the edges of the pastry with a little water. Fold the pastry over to enclose the filling and press down to seal. Crimp the edge to secure the filling. Repeat with the remaining pastry and filling.

9 In a deep-fryer or a large heavy-based saucepan, heat the vegetable oil to 180°C (350°F) – a pinch of flour dropped into the oil should sizzle on contact – and deep-fry the pastries in batches for 8–10 minutes, until golden brown. Remove from the oil with a slotted spoon and drain on paper towel before serving.

Moo ping

Grilled pork skewers

In Bangkok, where the morning rush is intense (and a fact of life), people usually get their breakfast from street-food vendors. Moo ping is a favourite, as it's rarely prepared at home due to its long marination time and involved cooking process, and it is readily available on the streets during the morning hours. The pork is marinated in aromatic spices and barbecued over charcoal before being served hot, usually with sticky rice. Don't be tempted to substitute the fattier pork loin for another cut, as the juicy tenderness of the loin is the best part of moo ping.

Makes 10

40 g (1½ oz) garlic cloves, peeled

20 g (¾ oz) coriander (cilantro) roots, scraped clean

5 g (¼ oz) whole white peppercorns

1.2 kg (2 lb 10 oz) pork loin, cut into 5 mm (¼ in) slices

250 ml (8½ fl oz/1 cup) evaporated milk

125 ml (4 fl oz/½ cup) coconut milk

80 ml (2½ fl oz/⅓ cup) soy sauce

½ teaspoon dark soy sauce

80 ml (2½ fl oz/⅓ cup) Maggi seasoning

70 ml (2¼ fl oz) grapeseed oil

cooked sticky rice, to serve

1 Using a mortar and pestle, pound the garlic, coriander roots and white peppercorns into a paste. Transfer the paste to a large, non-reactive bowl and add all of the remaining ingredients except the sticky rice, mixing well to combine. Cover and place in the refrigerator to marinate for at least a few hours, preferably overnight.

2 If using bamboo skewers, soak them in water for 2 hours before cooking to prevent them from burning.

3 Thread 4–6 slices of marinated pork onto each skewer. Reserve the marinade for grilling.

4 Using a charcoal barbecue (grill), cook the pork skewers over low heat, frequently brushing both sides with the marinade, for 10–15 minutes, until the pork is cooked. Alternatively, if you don't have a charcoal barbecue, you can cook the skewers on a gas barbecue or in a chargrill pan or non-stick frying pan on your stovetop.

5 Serve hot with cooked sticky rice.

ROTI MATABA
Stuffed roti

Roti mataba comes from the Muslim communities of southern Thailand, and also has its roots in India, where roti is a staple. Although not considered to be a 'traditional' Thai food, roti has been eaten by Thais for as long as anyone can remember, and dates back to the fourteenth century, when migrants from Malaysia and India arrived, along with their cuisines. In this variation on roti, the flatbread is stuffed with spiced minced (ground) meat and vegetables, then pan-fried until golden. Somewhat rare in Bangkok, roti mataba can only be found in a few famous places that specialise in this southern Thai delicacy. The sweet version of roti, however, is more common, with street vendors selling roti topped with popular options such as sweetened condensed milk and banana.

The roti dough has to be rested overnight, so this recipe is best prepared the day before.

Makes 4

70 ml (2¼ oz) grapeseed oil, plus extra for greasing and frying

½ tablespoon unsalted butter

1 tablespoon Three-spice paste (page 194)

1½ teaspoons curry powder

1 onion, diced

200 g (7 oz) minced (ground) chicken

½ tablespoon caster (superfine) sugar

fine sea salt, to taste

3 eggs, beaten

3 spring onions (scallions), finely sliced

Cucumber relish (page 194), to serve

Roti dough

vegetable oil, for greasing

300 g (10½ oz) plain (all-purpose) flour

40 ml (1¼ fl oz) evaporated milk or full-cream (whole) milk

1 teaspoon fine sea salt

1 egg

15 g (½ oz) ghee or butter

1 First, make the roti dough. Lightly grease a baking tray with the vegetable oil and set aside. Place the flour in a large bowl or in the bowl of a stand mixer with a dough hook attachment and make a well in the centre. In a separate bowl, thoroughly whisk together the milk, salt, egg and 130 ml (4½ fl oz) water. Pour the mixture into the well in the centre of the flour and mix until a dough begins to form. Add the ghee and knead for 5 minutes, until the dough becomes smooth and elastic. Cover and set aside to rest for 20 minutes.

2 Divide the dough into four equal portions. Grease your fingers with a little vegetable oil and shape the portions into balls. Place the dough balls on the greased baking tray, cover with plastic wrap or muslin (cheesecloth) and refrigerate overnight.

3 Heat the oil and butter in a large non-stick frying pan over medium–high heat. Add the three-spice paste and curry powder and stir until fragrant. Sauté the onion until translucent, then add the chicken and stir-fry for 5 minutes, or until the chicken is browned and cooked through. Add the caster sugar and season with salt to taste. Remove from the heat and set aside.

4 Remove the dough balls from the refrigerator 10–15 minutes before you plan to assemble the roti mataba. Grease your work surface and fingers with oil, then place a dough ball onto the work surface and flatten it out with your hands into a sheet roughly 2 mm (1/16 in) thick and three times as wide as it is long. Spread one-quarter of the chicken filling over the centre third of the dough sheet, top with 3 tablespoons of beaten egg and sprinkle with one-quarter of the sliced spring onion. Fold the left and right thirds of the dough sheet over the filling to create a square package and press the edges to seal. Repeat with the remaining dough balls and filling.

5 Heat a little grapeseed oil in a large non-stick frying pan over medium heat. Working with one parcel at a time, pan-fry the roti mataba for 2–3 minutes on each side, until crisp and golden brown on both sides. Transfer to a serving plate and serve hot with cucumber relish.

KHAI LUK KHEUY

Son-in-law eggs

What is the story behind the name of this famous Thai dish? There are many origin tales (some involving a displeased mother-in-law wanting to send a message), but the truth is lost to history. For such a legendary dish, khai luk kheuy is a simple one: boiled eggs, fried until a crisp golden skin forms, served with tamarind sauce. It is surprisingly sweet, but this sweetness is offset by irresistibly savoury fried shallots, and it is delicious when eaten with rice. Khai luk keuy is simple to cook at home and is also a common fixture among the street-food stalls and markets of Bangkok. This recipe calls for duck eggs, but chicken eggs also work well.

Serves 2

4 duck eggs

250 ml (8½ fl oz/1 cup) grapeseed oil

3 red shallots, finely sliced

4 dried red chillies

2 tablespoons grated palm sugar

3 tablespoons tamarind concentrate

1 tablespoon fish sauce

coriander (cilantro) leaves, to garnish

steamed jasmine rice, to serve

1 Fill a large bowl with iced water and set aside. Bring a saucepan of water to the boil over high heat and boil the eggs for 6 minutes. Using a slotted spoon, transfer the eggs to the iced water. Once the eggs are cool, peel them and set aside.

2 Heat the oil in a wok or a frying pan with deep sides over low–medium heat and gently fry the shallots and dried chillies until the shallots are golden brown and crisp. Remove the shallots and chillies from the oil with a slotted spoon and set aside to drain on paper towel.

3 Increase the heat to medium and fry the peeled eggs in the same oil for 2 minutes, or until golden all over. Remove the eggs from the oil with a slotted spoon and set aside to drain on paper towel.

4 Remove all but 3–4 tablespoons of oil from the wok and reduce the heat to low. Add the palm sugar and cook until it melts, caramelises and turns a rich brown, taking care not to let it burn. Mix in the tamarind concentrate and fish sauce and continue to stir for 10 minutes, until the sauce thickens slightly.

5 Slice the eggs in half lengthways and arrange on a serving plate. Spoon the sauce over the eggs and sprinkle with the fried shallots and chillies. Garnish with a few coriander leaves and serve with steamed jasmine rice.

Rice

Rice has been a part of Thai culture for centuries. It is the most essential ingredient in Thai cuisine and contributes significantly to the country's economy and exports. In the past, rice was traditionally harvested by hand, and was highly valued as farmers had to work under extreme conditions during harvest. The introduction of modern machinery and farming techniques improved working conditions and made harvesting rice less labour-intensive, which not only led to increased rice production, but also made it more affordable.

The most common types of rice served up at Thai dining tables are long-grain rice (such as jasmine rice) and glutinous rice. Long-grain rice is the general preference in most parts of Thailand, but glutinous rice is eaten on a regular basis in the north and especially the northeast, where the regional cuisine is highly influenced by neighbouring Laos.

Rice is essential to mealtimes in Thailand, and dishes such as curries or soups are incomplete without it. It is the main ingredient in khao tom (rice soup) and jok (congee), the Chinese-influenced dishes that are a favourite for breakfast and late-night suppers. Khao

niaow, or sweetened glutinous rice soaked in coconut milk and served with fresh fruit is one of the most popular Thai desserts, while khao taen, a crispy rice cracker topped with palm sugar syrup, is another well-known snack. Ground toasted rice is used to add flavour and texture to laap, the famous salad from northeastern Thailand, as well as to make dipping sauce to complement gai yang (grilled chicken). The Thais even ferment white glutinous rice to make khao mak, an ancient fermented rice dessert. From breakfast and lunch to late-night sweet treats, when it comes to rice, the Thais really have no limitations on when and how to eat it.

JOK

Rice porridge with pork meatballs and soft-boiled egg

A warming savoury rice porridge, jok, or congee, is a common breakfast and late-night supper in Thailand. The origin of the dish is unclear, but it is thought to have its roots in the country's Chinese population. Available widely on the streets and in markets, jok is usually made from broken rice that has been cooked for a long time until smooth, then served with various accompaniments, with the most common being minced pork and soft-boiled egg. Although a common dish, jok requires a long time to cook and is taken seriously by the Thais. There are certain popular spots specialising in jok with interesting ingredients, such as pork offal or seafood, which attract the locals from morning to late at night.

Serves 4

450 g (1 lb) jasmine rice

3 litres (3 quarts) Pork stock (page 192), plus extra if necessary

fine sea salt, to taste

4 eggs

freshly ground white pepper, to serve

1 tablespoon sesame oil

2 spring onions (scallions), finely chopped

15 g (½ oz) young ginger, peeled and julienned

coriander (cilantro) leaves, to garnish

Pork meatballs

5 garlic cloves, peeled

10 whole white peppercorns

400 g (14 oz) minced (ground) pork

2 tablespoons soy sauce

1 tablespoon caster (superfine) sugar

½ teaspoon bicarbonate of soda (baking soda)

1 First, prepare the pork meatballs. In a mortar and pestle, pound the garlic and white peppercorns into a fine paste. Add the minced pork and pound until homogenised, then add the remaining meatball ingredients and mix well. Cover and set aside in the refrigerator to marinate for a minimum of 3 hours.

2 Meanwhile, rinse the rice once or twice and strain through a mesh sieve to remove excess moisture. Using a blender or a mortar and pestle, process or pound the rice to a medium–fine consistency.

3 In a large stockpot or saucepan over high heat, combine the broken rice and pork stock and bring to the boil. Reduce the heat to low and simmer, stirring constantly to prevent the rice from sticking to the bottom of the pot, until the mixture becomes creamy. If the jok is too thick, add more pork stock or water as needed.

4 Take 1 tablespoon of the marinated pork mixture and roll it into a meatball using wet hands, repeating the process until all of the pork has been used. Add the meatballs to the jok and simmer for 10–15 minutes, until the meatballs are cooked through. Season with salt to taste.

5 Bring a saucepan half-filled with water to the boil over high heat. Remove from the heat and allow to cool for 1 minute. Place the eggs in the saucepan and leave uncovered for 12 minutes. Using a slotted spoon, transfer the eggs to a bowl of cold or iced water to cool for a minimum of 5 minutes.

6 Divide the jok among four bowls and crack an egg into each one. Garnish with white pepper, sesame oil, spring onion, ginger and coriander leaves, to taste.

Gaeng jeut luk rok

Egg sausage soup

Luk rok is egg sausage, an ancient way of preparing eggs similar to making regular sausages, except that the sausage casings (typically pork intestines) are filled with seasoned beaten egg instead of meat. The luk rok is poached, then cut into small, springy pieces and further cooked in a fragrant savoury soup filled with prawns or other protein. Although gaeng jeut luk rok is a uniquely Thai dish, it is slowly disappearing from the country's culinary scene.

Serves 2–4

1 litre (1 quart/4 cups) Pork stock (page 192)

¾ teaspoon whole black peppercorns, toasted

3 coriander (cilantro) roots, scraped clean and finely chopped

7 garlic cloves, finely chopped

2 tablespoons fish sauce

1½ teaspoons oyster sauce

200 g (7 oz) tiger prawns (shrimp), peeled and deveined, tails left intact

10 dried daylily flowers (golden needles), soaked and drained (see glossary)

coriander (cilantro) leaves, to garnish

Egg sausage

1 × 40 cm (15¾ in) natural pork sausage casing

70 g (2½ oz) fine sea salt (optional)

3 eggs

3 duck egg yolks

1 tablespoon fish sauce

1 First, prepare the egg sausage. If the natural casing hasn't been thoroughly cleaned beforehand, rub it all over with the salt and rinse both the outside and the inside twice. Tie a double knot at one end of the casing and set aside.

2 Beat the eggs and the fish sauce together until thoroughly combined. Pass the mixture through a mesh sieve twice to remove any lumps and transfer to a pitcher or a bowl with a pouring lip.

3 Insert the narrow end of a funnel into the untied end of the casing. Holding the casing tight around the funnel, fill with the egg mixture and close off with a double knot.

4 Place the egg sausage in a large saucepan filled with water. Bring to a gentle simmer over very low heat and cook for 2 hours, never allowing the water to come to the boil. The sausage is cooked when you can pierce it with a toothpick without any egg mixture leaking out. Fill a large bowl with iced water and transfer the cooked sausage to the bowl using a slotted spoon. Once cool, cut into 2–4 cm (¾–1½ in) lengths and set aside.

5 Bring the pork stock to the boil in a saucepan over medium heat. Meanwhile, in a mortar and pestle, pound the peppercorns, coriander root and garlic into a fine paste. Add the paste to the boiling stock, along with the fish sauce and oyster sauce.

6 Cook the prawns in the stock until they begin to change colour, then add the daylily flowers and egg sausage pieces. Bring the stock to the boil again before removing from the heat. Serve garnished with coriander leaves.

NAM TAO HOO
Soy milk

Thai people consider nam tao hoo, or soy milk, to be a very healthy breakfast or late-night snack. Introduced to Thailand by Chinese migrants, it can be served hot or cold, is usually accompanied by various additions, such as pearl barley, sago and grass jelly, and is typically sweetened. It is also sold on the streets with Chinese doughnuts: a perfect breakfast combination.

Serves 6

250 g (9 oz) split soybeans

5 pandan leaves, coarsely chopped

2 litres (2 quarts) filtered water

100 g (3½ oz) caster (superfine) sugar

½ teaspoon fine sea salt, plus extra if necessary

1 Place the soybeans in a colander and rinse well under running water until the water runs clear. Discard any discoloured beans, loose hulls or grit and transfer to a large bowl. Soak the beans in 1 litre (1 quart/4 cups) water for a minimum of 5 hours, but for no longer than 10 hours. Drain the soybeans, rinse under running water and drain again.

2 Place the soybeans, pandan leaves and filtered water in a blender and blend until smooth. Strain the liquid through a piece of muslin (cheesecloth) into a large saucepan, squeezing out as much of the liquid as you can. Discard the leftover pulp.

3 Bring the liquid to the boil over medium heat and cook, stirring constantly, for 5 minutes. Reduce the heat to low and add the caster sugar and salt, stirring until dissolved. Taste and add more sugar or salt if necessary. Remove from the heat and serve hot or cold.

KHANOM PEUAK TOD

Fried taro cakes

Although the name suggests this dish might be a dessert, it is in fact a savoury snack served with a sweet and sour dipping sauce. Khanom peuak tod is widely sold around Bangkok during the Nine Emperor Gods Festival, a Taoist celebration that begins on the ninth lunar month of the Chinese calendar and is an important festival in the Thai–Chinese community. For nine days, participants in the festival avoid eating meat, seafood and dairy. The festival is also observed by Chinese communities in other Southeast Asian countries, such as Malaysia, Indonesia and Singapore.

Serves 4

175 g (6 oz/1 cup) rice flour

150 g (5½ oz/1 cup) plain (all-purpose) flour

250 ml (8½ fl oz/1 cup) coconut milk

130 g (4½ oz/¾ cup) cooked black beans

½ taro root, peeled and sliced into sticks

1 teaspoon fine sea salt

250 ml (8½ fl oz/1 cup) vegetable oil, for deep-frying

Dipping sauce

1½ tablespoons tamarind concentrate

3 tablespoons grated palm sugar

2 red chillies, crushed

1 tablespoon coarsely chopped peanuts

1 First, make the dipping sauce. In a small saucepan over medium heat, combine the tamarind concentrate, palm sugar and 250 ml (8½ fl oz/1 cup) water, stirring until the sugar dissolves and the mixture thickens slightly. Remove from the heat and check for seasoning; the flavour should be a balance of sweet and sour. Add more tamarind concentrate or palm sugar if necessary, then add the chilli and stir to combine. Pour into small serving bowls, sprinkle with the peanuts and set aside.

2 Combine all of the ingredients except the salt and oil in a bowl. Pour in 250 ml (8½ fl oz/1 cup) water, mix well, then stir in the salt.

3 Heat the oil in a wok or a deep heavy-based saucepan over medium heat until a cube of bread dropped into the oil browns in 30 seconds – approximately 190°C (375°F). Dip a ladle into the oil to coat the inside of the bowl portion with hot oil.

4 Place a large spoonful of the taro batter into the oiled ladle and carefully lower the ladle into the hot oil. Fry for 5–7 minutes, until the batter turns golden and floats away from the ladle to the surface. Remove with a slotted spoon and drain on paper towel. Repeat with the remaining batter.

5 Serve warm with the dipping sauce.

Khanom Gui Chai

Chive cakes

Like Fried taro cakes (page 35), khanom gui chai is a savoury dish with a name that suggests sweetness. They are commonly found in markets and at street-food stalls in Bangkok, and are thought to have arrived with Chinese merchants in the nineteenth century, becoming popular among locals after the Second World War. There are a few variations: cakes that are shaped differently and filled with ingredients such as bamboo shoots, taro or jicama (yam bean). This version, a sweet-savoury chive filling wrapped in a chewy dough made from tapioca flour, is the most popular one.

Makes 12

125 g (4½ oz) rice flour, plus extra for dusting

1 teaspoon white glutinous rice flour

160 g (5½ oz) tapioca flour

450 ml (15 fl oz) boiling water

30 ml (1 fl oz) vegetable oil, plus extra for brushing

Chive filling

500 g (1 lb 2 oz) garlic chives, sliced into 1 cm (½ in) lengths

1 tablespoon fine sea salt

100 g (3½ oz) caster (superfine) sugar

1 tablespoon bicarbonate of soda (baking soda)

160 ml (5½ fl oz) grapeseed oil

Dipping sauce

200 ml (7 fl oz) dark soy sauce

125 ml (4 fl oz/½ cup) white vinegar

1 teaspoon fine sea salt

100 g (3½ oz) caster (superfine) sugar

2 tablespoons coarsely pounded red chillies

2 tablespoons coarsely pounded garlic cloves

1 First, prepare the chive filling. In a large mixing bowl, combine all of the ingredients and squeeze the chives until they soften. Alternatively, you can use a stand mixer with a beater attachment and work the chives on high speed for 2 minutes. Strain the chives through a mesh sieve to remove the liquid and set aside.

2 To prepare the dipping sauce, heat 200 ml (7 fl oz) water and all the ingredients except the chilli and garlic in a small saucepan over low heat until the salt and sugar dissolve. Set aside to cool.

3 In the bowl of a stand mixer with a beater attachment, combine the rice flours and 100 g (3½ oz) of the tapioca flour. Add the boiling water to the mixture and beat on high speed until the consistency resembles a thick glue and there are no dry lumps of flour left. Set aside to cool to room temperature.

4 Once the mixture has cooled, add the vegetable oil and the remaining tapioca flour and mix on low speed until the oil has been incorporated into the dough. With the mixer still running, slowly add 45 ml (1½ fl oz) water and continue

to mix for 3 minutes, or until the dough is shiny and has no spring to it – pressing your finger into the dough should leave an indentation that doesn't bounce back.

5 Pinch off a 2–3 cm (¾–1¼ in) diameter piece of the dough and dust with a little rice flour. On a clean work surface, roll out the piece of dough with a rolling pin until you have a disc 5 mm–1 cm (¼–½ in) thick and 7 cm (2¾ in) in diameter.

6 Place 1 heaped tablespoon of chive filling in the centre of the disc and gather the edges together so that you have a round parcel. Pinch to seal and repeat with the remaining dough and filling.

7 Bring a large saucepan of water to the boil over high heat. Place the chive cakes in the bottom of a large bamboo steamer lined with baking paper or a plastic steaming sheet, leaving space between each one. Steam for 5 minutes, then brush the top of each cake with a little vegetable oil. Finally, add the chilli and garlic to the dipping sauce and serve with the warm chive cakes.

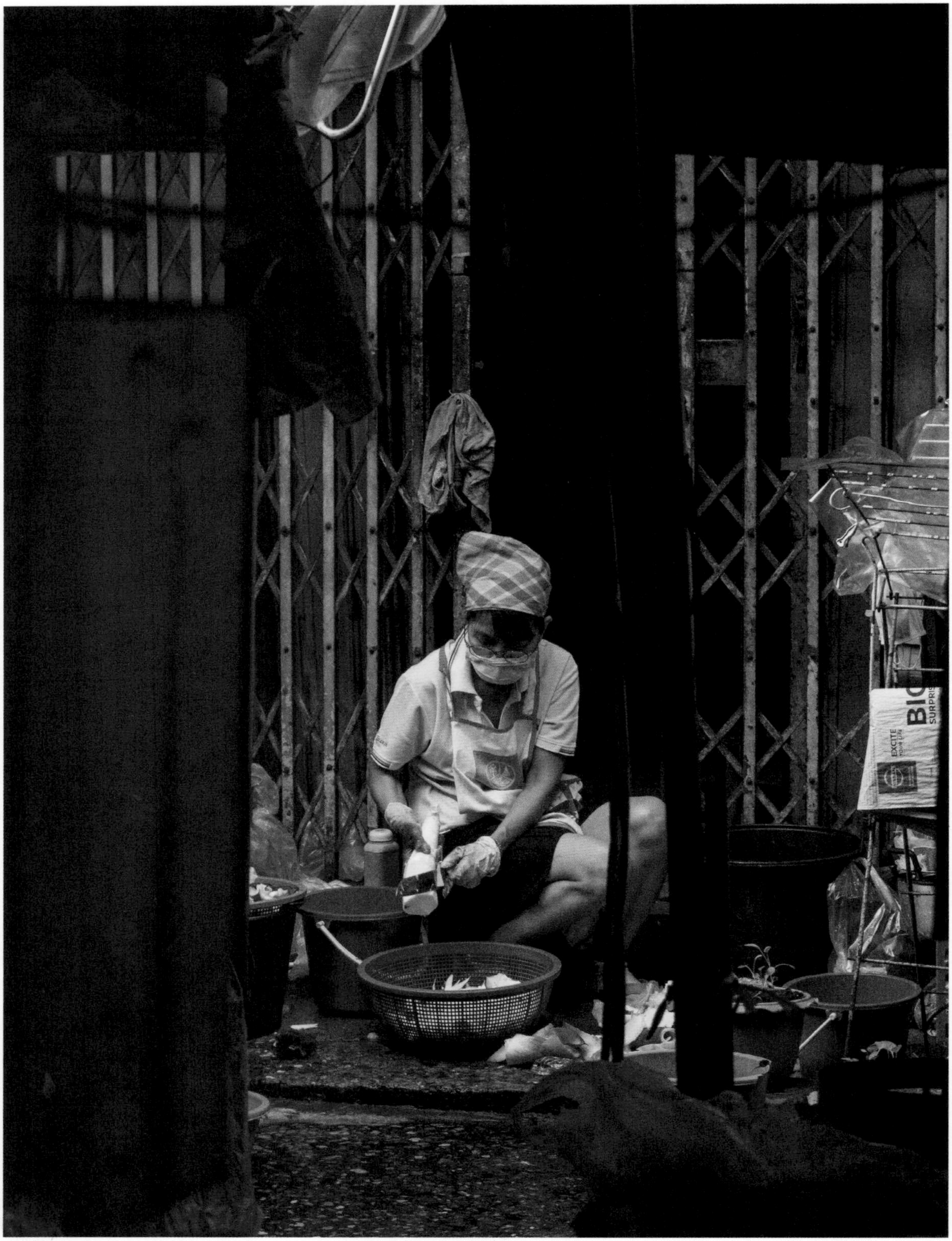

Khai toon

Steamed egg custard

Khai toon is probably one of the most common breakfasts to cook at home in Thailand. A silky-smooth savoury egg custard, it is simple and fast to make, yet it is nutritious and has a delicate flavour. This recipe calls for shiitake mushrooms and prawns (shrimp), but these toppings can be adjusted to your liking.

Serves 2

7 banana prawns (shrimp), peeled

1 tablespoon minced (ground) pork

3 eggs, beaten

1 tablespoon sliced spring onion (scallion)

¼ teaspoon ground white pepper

1 tablespoon soy sauce

1 tablespoon oyster sauce

½ tablespoon grapeseed oil

2 shiitake mushrooms

1 Using a sharp knife, coarsely mince three of the prawns. Place in a mixing bowl with the pork and beaten egg and whisk to combine. Add the spring onion, white pepper, soy sauce, oyster sauce and oil, and mix well. Divide the egg mixture between two small soup bowls and cover with foil.

2 Fill a large saucepan with water, place a large bamboo steamer on top and bring to the boil over medium heat. Place the bowls in the steamer, cover and reduce the heat to low. Steam for 5 minutes, then remove the foil and top each custard with a shiitake mushroom and two peeled prawns. Replace the foil and steam for a further 5 minutes, or until a skewer inserted into the centre of the custard comes out clean.

3 Serve the custards warm in their bowls.

SHIITAKE

KHANOM TUNG DTAK

Poor man's pancakes

One of Thailand's traditional desserts, found at local markets and events in temples all over the country, khanom tung dtak is becoming harder to find these days. The name is a clue to its supposed origin: these 'poor man's pancakes' were once sold as a cheap snack at boxing matches and horse races, and were favoured by those who had lost their money on bad bets. The perfect pancake should have a crisp outer skin and a soft centre, with fillings ranging from custard or shredded coconut to sesame seeds.

Serves 4

130 g (4½ oz/¾ cup) rice flour

65 g (2¼ oz) plain (all-purpose) flour

1 tablespoon dried yeast

50 g (1¾ oz) caster (superfine) sugar

½ teaspoon baking powder

vegetable oil or butter, for greasing

Coconut filling

1 tablespoon white sesame seeds

1 tablespoon black sesame seeds

2 tablespoons brown sugar

100 g (3½ oz) unsweetened shredded coconut

1 In a large mixing bowl, combine the flours, yeast and caster sugar and make a well in the centre. Pour 360 ml (12 fl oz) lukewarm water into the well and stir to incorporate. Cover with a tea towel and leave to rest at room temperature for 30 minutes. After resting, add the baking powder and mix well.

2 To prepare the filling, dry-fry the sesame seeds in a small frying pan over medium heat until the white sesame seeds are golden brown and fragrant. Transfer to a bowl, add the brown sugar and stir to combine. Set aside.

3 Heat a non-stick frying pan with a lid over medium heat and lightly grease with vegetable oil or butter. Ladle one-quarter of the batter into the pan, tilting it so that the batter evenly coats the whole surface. Cover and cook for 4–5 minutes, checking often, until the bottom is brown and crisp and the top is firm.

4 Add one-quarter of the shredded coconut to the centre of the pancake, sprinkle with one-quarter of the filling mixture and fold the pancake in half to create a semicircle. Transfer to a plate and keep warm. Repeat with the remaining ingredients and serve hot.

GLUAY TOD

Fried bananas

Gluay tod is usually eaten for breakfast, but it's also a common snack at any time of day in Thailand, as well as in other Southeast Asian countries. Often sold by street vendors, bananas (other fruits and vegetables, such as taro or potatoes, are also used in some places) are dipped in a sweet batter and deep-fried until golden brown and crisp. A popular takeaway snack among Bangkok locals, gluay tod is a perfect on-the-road late-afternoon treat. Certain busy streets in Bangkok are now home to vendors who sell their fried bananas in white paper bags, easily recognisable to drivers waiting at traffic lights. These are best enjoyed hot, while the batter is crisp and the banana is soft and gooey.

Makes 15 pieces

2 tablespoons white sesame seeds

70 g (2½ oz) rice flour

20 g (¾ oz) plain (all-purpose) flour

50 g (1¾ oz) palm sugar, finely grated

1½ teaspoons fine sea salt

125 ml (4 fl oz/½ cup) Limewater (page 190)

70 g (2½ oz) unsweetened shredded coconut

5 lady finger bananas

250 ml (8½ fl oz/1 cup) vegetable oil, for deep-frying

1 In a small frying pan over medium heat, dry-fry the sesame seeds until golden brown and fragrant. Transfer to a bowl and set aside.

2 In a large mixing bowl, combine the flours, palm sugar and salt. Add the limewater and stir well until there are no lumps, then fold in the shredded coconut and toasted sesame seeds.

3 Peel the bananas and cut them lengthways into thirds.

4 Heat the oil in a wok or a deep heavy-based saucepan over medium heat until a cube of bread dropped into the oil browns in 30 seconds – approximately 190°C (375°F). Working in batches, dip the sliced banana in the batter and deep-fry until golden. Remove the fried banana with a slotted spoon and drain on paper towel. Serve warm.

sangkaya Fak Tong

Pumpkin and coconut custard

In Thai, sangkaya means 'coconut custard', while fak tong means 'pumpkin'. Put them together and you have a delicious dessert that is high in vitamins and fibre. A coconut-custard filling is steamed in a whole pumpkin, creating a rich and creamy flavour and texture contrast. Sangkaya fak tong is widely available at local markets around Bangkok; our favourite is from Aor Tor Kor market. It's really easy to cook at home, and while you might be tempted to use chicken eggs, make sure you use duck eggs for the best results.

Serves 5

1 × 1 kg (2 lb 3 oz) pumpkin (squash)

4 duck eggs

200 g (7 oz) grated palm sugar or brown sugar

1 teaspoon fine sea salt

250 ml (8½ fl oz/1 cup) coconut cream

35 g (1¼ oz) rice flour

3 pandan leaves

1 Rinse the pumpkin thoroughly to remove any dirt. Using a sharp knife, carefully cut around the stem, remove the top and set it aside. Scoop out and discard the seeds and any soft, fibrous flesh. Set aside.

2 In a large mixing bowl, gently whisk the eggs, palm sugar and salt until smooth and creamy. Add the coconut cream and rice flour, mixing well to break up any lumps, followed by the pandan leaves. Lightly squeeze the pandan leaves to help extract the flavour.

3 Strain the custard through a fine sieve into a large heatproof bowl. Return the pandan leaves to the custard and discard anything else left in the sieve.

4 Bring a saucepan of water to the boil over medium heat. Place the bowl of custard on top of the saucepan to create a double-boiler, ensuring that the bottom of the bowl does not touch the water.

Cook, stirring continuously, until the custard thickens slightly, or reaches 70°C (158°F) on a sugar thermometer. Remove the pandan leaves from the custard and discard.

5 Pour the custard into the pumpkin until it reaches just below the rim, then replace the top of the pumpkin.

6 Fill a large saucepan with water, top with a bamboo steamer large enough to fit the pumpkin and bring to the boil over medium heat. Place the pumpkin in the steamer and steam for 45 minutes, or until the pumpkin is cooked all the way through and the custard is set. Remove from the heat and allow to cool to room temperature, then transfer to the refrigerator if not serving immediately.

7 To serve, cut the pumpkin into quarters or smaller wedges. Sangkaya fak tong is usually eaten at room temperature, but you can also serve it cold.

Khanom tua paep

Sweet mung bean dumplings

A Thai sweet made for special occasions and religious ceremonies, khanom tua paep can also be eaten for breakfast or as a morning snack. The dumpling skin is made with glutinous rice flour, which lends it a soft, chewy texture. Like Poor man's pancakes (page 40), these dumplings have become one of the rarer Thai desserts, and can usually only be found at local markets.

Serves 2

50 g (1¾ oz) yellow mung beans, soaked overnight and drained

50 g (1¾ oz) fresh or dried unsweetened shredded coconut

2 tablespoons white sesame seeds

3 tablespoons caster (superfine) sugar

¼ teaspoon fine sea salt

Pastry

65 g (2¼ oz) white glutinous rice flour

32 g (1¼ oz) black glutinous rice flour

125 ml (4 fl oz/½ cup) Perfumed water (page 190)

1 Fill a saucepan with water, place a bamboo steamer on top and bring to the boil over medium heat. Place the mung beans in the steamer and steam for 40 minutes, then add the shredded coconut and steam for a further 5 minutes. Remove from the heat, transfer the mung beans and shredded coconut to separate bowls and set aside to cool.

2 In a small frying pan over medium heat, dry-fry the sesame seeds until golden brown and fragrant. Transfer to a small bowl and combine with the caster sugar and salt. Set aside.

3 To make the pastry, sift the flours into a mixing bowl and whisk to combine. Sprinkle with the perfumed water and gently knead to form a soft, smooth dough. Pinch off pieces of the dough and shape into balls approximately 2 cm (¾ in) in diameter.

4 On a clean work surface, roll the dough out into discs approximately 5 mm (¼ in) thick and 4 cm (1½ in) in diameter. Place 2 teaspoons of the mung beans in the centre of a disc and wrap the dough around the filling, pinching the edges together to seal so that you have a roughly oval package. Set aside on a plate or tray and repeat with the remaining pastry and filling.

5 Fill a large bowl with water and bring a large saucepan of water to the boil over medium heat. Carefully add the dumplings to the boiling water and cook for approximately 5 minutes, or until the dumplings float to the surface. Using a slotted spoon, remove the cooked dumplings from the saucepan and transfer to the bowl of water to prevent them from sticking together.

6 To serve, sprinkle the dumplings with the sesame seed mixture and the shredded coconut.

KHANOM KROK
Coconut custard cupcakes

This is an ancient Thai dessert that can still be found on the streets of Bangkok today. Popular in Thailand since the beginning of the Ayutthaya period (1351–1767), this delicacy is topped with various unexpected ingredients, such as chives, corn and taro. The cupcakes are best eaten warm, while the bottoms are still crisp and the middles retain their soft custard-like texture. Khanom krok is cooked on the stovetop in a special frying pan with spherical indentations, similar to a Danish Æbelskiver pan, Dutch poffertje pan or Japanese takoyaki pan. If you're unable to find a khanom krok pan (or one of its cousins), small stainless steel moulds placed in a frying pan can be used instead.

Serves 5

200 g (7 oz) rice flour

50 g (1¾ oz) white glutinous rice flour

1 teaspoon fine sea salt

1 tablespoon caster (superfine) sugar

360 ml (12 fl oz) coconut cream

3 tablespoons vegetable oil, for greasing

3 spring onions (scallions), 2 tablespoons sweet corn kernels or small bunch chives, finely chopped, to serve

Filling

1 tablespoon rice flour

1 teaspoon salt

65 g (2¼ oz) caster (superfine) sugar

360 ml (12 fl oz) coconut cream

1 In a large mixing bowl, combine the rice flours, salt and caster sugar. Slowly add the coconut cream to the dry ingredients, followed by 360 ml (12 fl oz) hot water, stirring with a whisk as you go, until you have a smooth batter. Set aside.

2 To make the filling, combine the rice flour, salt and caster sugar in a mixing bowl, then whisk in the coconut cream and stir until the sugar has dissolved. Set aside.

3 Grease a khanom krok pan with the vegetable oil and place over medium heat until a small amount of batter dropped into the pan immediately sizzles. Stir the batter to mix well, then pour into the indentations until each one is two-thirds full. Stir the filling to mix well, then gently pour on top of the batter until each of the indentations is full. Cover the pan with a lid and cook for 5 minutes, until the filling is set, then remove the khanom krok from the indentations with a spoon and transfer to a serving plate.

4 Sprinkle the khanom krok with spring onion, corn or chives and serve while still warm.

M

D

MID

As lunchtime approaches, Bangkok's streets come back to life with more street-food hawkers, offering a slightly different selection from what's available at breakfast – lunch is when curries and spicy dishes really show up on menus. People take a moment to enjoy their food, gathering around dining tables with friends and colleagues, although single dishes, rather than shared meals, are more common at lunch, as time is still a factor. Ahan tam sang ('food to order') stalls pop up around the city; these vendors have a near-magical ability to create almost any common Thai dish you can think of, from soups and noodles to curries and stir-fries. Ahan tam sang menus vary from stall to stall, and only the locals know who offers what.

Thai people love to eat and they graze throughout the day; lunch is always followed by snacks and fresh fruit, while young people visit their favourite cafés for coffee and afternoon tea. Strolling through the streets, you will often spot vendors pushing carts stacked with fresh fruit. These fruit stalls can be found all over Bangkok, offering up tropical fruit such as

mango, pineapple and guava with salt and chilli for dipping. Fruit stalls are truly a Bangkok icon and are the locals' pick for healthy nibbles.

In Bangkok's culinary melting pot, snacks also come in many other forms, from traditional Thai desserts to Western-style baked goods. Roti is a favourite – a dish originally from India that has been given a Thai twist with toppings such as banana and sweetened condensed milk. French pastries and cakes are widely available, especially in shopping centres, which are home to many franchise cafés and bakeries. Young Thai people generally favour these sweet treats over Thai desserts, so it is not surprising (but perhaps a little sad!) that traditional desserts are more difficult to find than croissants or muffins. That being said, visit one of the city's many markets and you can still find local sweet specialties, such as foi tong, an ancient egg yolk dessert, or khanom mor gaeng, a custard made with taro or mung bean.

Exploring Bangkok in the middle of the day is a delight for any food-lover – it's undeniable that the city's culinary offerings cater for every appetite.

KHAO PAD SAPPAROD

Pineapple fried rice

Khao pad, or fried rice, is the most flexible dish in Thai cuisine, with cooks able to switch up ingredients depending on what they have on hand. Like Egg noodles in chicken curry (page 88) and Crispy oyster omelette (page 126), khao pad originally came from China and first found popularity in the nineteenth century, when hawkers started selling the dish widely. The most important factors in perfecting this dish are the rice and the wok. The rice must be dry and at room temperature, and cooking it in a very hot wok ensures that the heat is evenly distributed and the rice gains a toasted flavour.

Serves 2

80 ml (2½ fl oz/⅓ cup) vegetable oil

2 garlic cloves, finely chopped

500 g (1 lb 2 oz) banana prawns (shrimp), peeled and deveined

1 red shallot, diced

400 g (14 oz) steamed jasmine rice, cooled (preferably from the previous day)

1 tablespoon soy sauce

1 tablespoon oyster sauce

1 tablespoon fish sauce

1 teaspoon caster (superfine) sugar

170 g (6 oz) fresh pineapple, cut into 2 cm (¾ in) cubes

1 spring onion (scallion), finely sliced

60 g (2 oz) roasted cashew nuts

1 tablespoon coriander (cilantro) leaves

2 lime wedges

1 Heat the oil in a wok over medium heat and stir-fry the garlic until fragrant. Increase the heat to high and add the prawns and shallot, stir-frying until the prawns are just cooked through.

2 Add the rice to the wok and stir-fry for 1–2 minutes, until the rice is well coated with oil. Season with the soy sauce, oyster sauce, fish sauce and caster sugar and stir-fry for 2–3 minutes. Add the pineapple, spring onion and cashew nuts and stir-fry for a further 1–2 minutes, until well combined. Remove from the heat and transfer to a serving bowl or a hollowed-out pineapple half.

3 To serve, sprinkle the khao pad sapparod with coriander leaves and accompany with the lime wedges.

KHAO PAD PU

Crab fried rice

This is another dish popular among most Thai children – something often ordered for the kids' table when dining out with the family. The rich, tender meat of the crab makes khao pad pu a special dish, but it is really very simple to cook at home and makes for a delicious lunch or dinner for any occasion.

Serves 2

80 ml (2½ fl oz/⅓ cup) vegetable oil

2 garlic cloves, finely chopped

1 egg

400 g (14 oz) steamed jasmine rice, cooled (preferably from the previous day)

1 tablespoon soy sauce

1 tablespoon oyster sauce

1 tablespoon fish sauce

1 teaspoon caster (superfine) sugar

½ teaspoon ground white pepper

2 spring onions (scallions), finely sliced

200 g (7 oz) cooked crab meat

1 tablespoon shredded coriander (cilantro) leaves

1 Heat the oil in a wok over high heat until it begins to shimmer. Add the garlic and stir-fry until fragrant and beginning to brown.

2 Crack the egg into the oil and allow it to firm up a little before stirring to break it up. Add the rice, reduce the heat to medium and stir-fry for 1–2 minutes, until the rice is well coated in the oil and the egg is distributed evenly. Season with the soy sauce, oyster sauce, fish sauce, caster sugar and white pepper, then add the spring onion and stir gently to combine.

3 Mix in almost all of the crab meat, setting aside a little for garnishing. Remove from the heat and transfer to a serving bowl.

4 Just before serving, sprinkle the khao pad pu with the coriander leaves and reserved crab meat.

Moo pad qing

Stir-fried pork with ginger

Moo pad qing is a simple comfort food familiar to every Thai household, and can be bought from food hawkers all around Bangkok, but it's not seen as much outside of the country. Requiring only a few ingredients (for Thai food, at least), moo pad qing is highly fragrant and is best enjoyed with steamed rice. As the highlight of this dish is ginger, it's vital to use young ginger for its fresher, milder flavour.

Serves 2

80 ml (2½ fl oz/⅓ cup) vegetable oil

3 garlic cloves, roughly chopped

1 × 8 cm (3¼ in) piece young ginger, julienned

2 red chillies, finely sliced

400 g (14 oz) pork loin, cut into 7 mm (¼ in) thick slices

1 tablespoon soy sauce

1 tablespoon fish sauce

2 tablespoons oyster sauce

1 teaspoon caster (superfine) sugar

100 g (3½ oz) wood ear fungus (see glossary)

1 teaspoon ground white pepper

1 spring onion (scallion), cut into 3 cm (1¼ in) lengths

steamed jasmine rice, to serve

1 Heat the oil in a wok over medium heat and stir-fry the garlic, ginger and chilli until fragrant. Add the pork and stir-fry for 4–5 minutes until almost cooked. Season with soy sauce, fish sauce, oyster sauce and caster sugar, add the wood ear fungus and stir to combine. Finally, add the ground white pepper and spring onion and stir-fry for 30 seconds.

2 Serve with steamed jasmine rice.

PLA MEUK GOONG GRATIEM PRIK THAI

Stir-fried baby octopus and prawns with garlic and black pepper

Pad gratiem prik thai is less well known outside Thailand, but it is a staple dish for Bangkok locals. Usually eaten with rice, it has an aromatic and spicy flavour profile thanks to the fried garlic and black pepper. This recipe calls for octopus and prawns (shrimp), but other protein sources such as chicken, beef or pork also work well.

Serves 2

100 ml (3½ fl oz) vegetable oil

6 garlic cloves, roughly chopped

2 coriander (cilantro) roots, scraped clean and finely sliced

400 g (14 oz) banana prawns (shrimp), peeled and deveined

100 g (3½ oz) baby octopus, cleaned and cut into 1 cm (½ in) slices

1 tablespoon soy sauce

1 tablespoon oyster sauce

pinch of fine sea salt

1 tablespoon freshly ground black pepper

steamed jasmine rice, to serve

1 Heat the oil in a wok over high heat and fry half the garlic until golden. Remove the garlic from the oil with a slotted spoon and set aside to drain on paper towel.

2 Using the leftover oil, sauté the coriander root and the remaining garlic until fragrant. Add the prawns and octopus and stir-fry until they begin to change colour.

3 Add the soy sauce, oyster sauce and salt. Stir-fry until the seafood is just cooked through and add the ground black pepper, stirring to combine. Remove from the heat, scatter with the fried garlic and serve warm with steamed jasmine rice.

COONG PAD PAK CAD KAO

Stir-fried cabbage with prawns

Another well-kept Thai culinary secret, this dish is well loved by home cooks and street-food stalls but underappreciated outside of the country. The recipe is simple: cabbage and prawns (shrimp) are stir-fried and caramelised with fish sauce, resulting in a dish rich in sweetness and umami flavour.

Serves 4

vegetable oil, for frying

50 g (1¾ oz) dried salted mackerel (see glossary)

5 garlic cloves, finely chopped

500 g (1 lb 2 oz) banana prawns (shrimp), peeled and deveined

300 g (10½ oz) green cabbage, cut into 6 cm (2¼ in) pieces

1 tablespoon fish sauce

1 tablespoon soy sauce

1 teaspoon oyster sauce

steamed jasmine rice, to serve

1 Place a wok over medium heat and add enough oil to half-cover the dried salted mackerel. Heat until a cube of bread dropped into the oil browns in 45 seconds – approximately 150°C (300°F). Add the mackerel and fry for 3–5 minutes on each side, until a deep golden brown. Remove from the oil with a slotted spoon and set aside to drain on paper towel. Once cool, shred the mackerel into small flakes and set aside. Discard all but 60 ml (2 fl oz/¼ cup) of the oil.

2 Return the oil to the heat and sauté the garlic until fragrant. Add the prawns and stir-fry until they begin to change colour. Add the cabbage and mackerel to the wok and stir-fry until the cabbage softens but still retains a little bite.

3 Add the fish sauce, soy sauce and oyster sauce and stir-fry to combine. Add 2 tablespoons water to the wok to deglaze, then remove from the heat.

4 Serve warm with steamed jasmine rice.

Pad Kana Moo GROB

Chinese broccoli with crispy pork

Pad kana moo grob has been a part of the Thai family meal for as long as anyone can remember. It is one of the most popular stir-fries ordered by locals at restaurants and street-food stalls, and is also often cooked at home. A simple dish, crispy pork belly is accompanied by the fresh green flavour of Chinese broccoli (gai lan), and is best enjoyed with jasmine rice and a side of crispy omelette.

You will need to start this recipe a day in advance.

Serves 2

400 g (14 oz) pork belly

1 tablespoon fine sea salt

80 ml (2½ fl oz/⅓ cup) vegetable oil

4 garlic cloves, roughly chopped

3 red bird's eye chillies, sliced

2 bunches Chinese broccoli (gai lan), finely sliced on the diagonal

100 g (3½ oz) shiitake mushrooms, cut into 5 mm (¼ in) slices

1 tablespoon oyster sauce

1 tablespoon soy sauce

1½ tablespoons fish sauce

1 teaspoon ground white pepper

steamed jasmine rice, to serve

Crispy omelette (page 195), to serve (optional)

1 Prepare the pork a day or two in advance. Using a sharp knife, score lines into the skin 5 mm (¼ in) apart, taking care not to cut into the meat. Place the pork on a piece of foil and fold the edges of the foil up around the meat, but not the skin. Transfer to the refrigerator and let the exposed skin air-dry for 1–2 days.

2 On the day of serving, preheat the oven to 220°C (430°F). Place the pork and the foil on a baking tray, sprinkle the pork skin with the salt and roast for 25–30 minutes, until the skin is crisp and golden and the meat is just cooked through. Remove from the oven and allow to rest, uncovered, for a minimum of 15 minutes.

3 Meanwhile, heat the oil in a wok over high heat. Sauté the garlic and chillies until fragrant. Add the Chinese broccoli and shiitake mushrooms and stir-fry for 2 minutes. Season with the oyster sauce, soy sauce and fish sauce and stir-fry for a further 2–3 minutes. Stir through the white pepper and remove from the heat.

4 Transfer the Chinese broccoli to a serving plate. Slice the pork belly and arrange on top of the Chinese broccoli. Serve with steamed jasmine rice and crispy omelette, if desired.

Pad kaphrao gai khai dao

Holy basil chicken with fried egg

Kaphrao, or holy basil, is one of the most commonly used herbs in Thai cuisine. Pad kaphrao – stir-fried basil – served with khai dao, or fried egg on rice, is the most popular quick lunch or dinner for Thais, and is often enjoyed at street-food stalls. Holy basil comes in two varieties in Thailand: red and white. The red variety, which grows in the wild, has purple stalks and is very pungent. The white variety, which is cultivated for consumption, has green stalks and a less intense flavour than the red. It's important to distinguish between the types of basil used in Thai cooking – holy basil (kaphrao), Thai basil (horapha) and hoary (lemon) basil (maenglak) – as they each have a distinctive flavour, and generally cannot be substituted for one another.

Serves 2

7 garlic cloves

5 bird's eye chillies

100 ml (3½ fl oz) vegetable oil

2 eggs

400 g (14 oz) minced (ground) chicken

2 tablespoons fish sauce

1 tablespoon oyster sauce

1 tablespoon soy sauce

1 teaspoon caster (superfine) sugar

1 long red chilli, sliced

25 g (1 oz/¾ cup loosely packed) holy basil leaves (see glossary)

steamed jasmine rice, to serve

Dipping sauce

2 red and green bird's eye chillies, very thinly sliced

2 tablespoons fish sauce

1 Using a mortar and pestle, pound the garlic cloves into a coarse paste, then add the chillies and pound them a few times to bruise them. If you prefer the stir-fry to be spicy, pound the chillies into a coarse paste. Set aside.

2 Heat the oil in a wok over medium heat until it begins to smoke. Fry the eggs in the oil until crisp, then remove from the wok with a slotted spoon and set aside to drain on paper towel.

3 Increase the heat to high. Using the leftover oil, stir-fry the garlic and chilli mixture until fragrant. Add the minced chicken and cook, stirring constantly to break it up, until the chicken is browned and almost cooked all the way through. Pour the fish sauce down the side of the wok, so that it pools beneath the chicken and allow it to cook, without stirring, for 1 minute, until caramelised.

4 Add the oyster sauce, soy sauce, caster sugar and long chilli and stir-fry to combine. Add 75 ml (2½ fl oz) water to the wok to deglaze, followed by the holy basil leaves. Stir-fry until the basil leaves are just wilted and remove from the heat.

5 To make the dipping sauce, combine the sliced chilli and the fish sauce.

6 Serve the pad kaphrao warm with steamed jasmine rice, the fried eggs and the dipping sauce.

KHAO KLUK GAPI

Rice seasoned with fermented shrimp paste

It's said that, once upon a time, rice and gapi (fermented shrimp paste) were essential travelling items for the Thai royal family. Khao kluk gapi is a traditional dish centred around those two key ingredients, and is a highly regarded dish in Thailand – so much so that a few special recipes from the royal family's kitchens have been made available to the public.

Serves 2–3

2 Chinese sausages (lap cheong), cut into 5 mm (¼ in) slices

170 ml (4¾ fl oz) vegetable oil

50 g (1¾ oz) dried shrimp (see glossary), soaked in warm water for 15 minutes and drained

3 eggs, beaten

5 garlic cloves, finely chopped

1 tablespoon gapi (fermented shrimp paste)

60 ml (2 fl oz/¼ cup) Pork stock (page 192) or water

500 g (1 lb 2 oz) steamed jasmine rice, cooled

Caramelised pork

80 ml (2½ fl oz/⅓ cup) vegetable oil

12 small red shallots, finely sliced

400 g (14 oz) pork belly, cut into 1 cm (½ in) cubes

2 tablespoons soy sauce

2 tablespoons oyster sauce

2 tablespoons dark soy sauce

200 g (7 oz) palm sugar, grated

To serve

1 sour green mango, julienned

2 small red shallots, finely sliced

30 g (1 oz/¼ cup) finely sliced snake (yard-long) beans

2–3 lime wedges

5 red and green bird's eye chillies, roughly chopped

1 First, prepare the caramelised pork. Heat the oil in a wok over medium heat and sauté the shallots until fragrant. Add the pork and stir-fry for 6–7 minutes, then stir in the remaining ingredients. Add 125 ml (4 fl oz/½ cup) water to the wok, reduce the heat to low–medium and cook for 5–10 minutes, until the liquid evaporates and the mixture caramelises and becomes sticky. Remove from the heat and set aside.

2 Bring a small saucepan of water to the boil over high heat and blanch the Chinese sausage for 2 minutes. Remove from the heat, drain and pat dry with paper towel. Heat 140 ml (4½ fl oz) of the oil in a clean wok over medium heat. Add the blanched Chinese sausage and fry for 2–3 minutes, until golden. Remove from the oil with a slotted spoon and set aside to drain on paper towel. Using the leftover oil, fry the shrimp for 2–3 minutes, until golden brown. Remove from the oil with a slotted spoon and set aside to drain on paper towel. Drain off the oil and reserve for frying.

3 Add 1 tablespoon of the reserved oil to the wok and return the wok to the heat. Tilt the wok so that the oil coats the base and side, then add one-third of the beaten egg and tilt the wok to create a thin omelette. Cook until set, then carefully transfer to a plate. Repeat the process with the reserved oil and remaining beaten egg so that you have three omelettes. Stack the omelettes on top of each other, cut them into quarters and slice them into 5 mm (¼ in) thick strips. Set aside. Discard any remaining reserved oil.

4 In a clean wok, heat the remaining 30 ml (1 fl oz) of the fresh oil over medium heat and sauté the garlic until golden and fragrant. Add the gapi, mashing it to remove any lumps, and fry for 2 minutes, until fragrant. Pour in the stock and stir until the gapi is dissolved, then add the rice and reduce the heat to low. Stir thoroughly to evenly distribute the gapi throughout the rice. Once the rice has changed colour and is hot, remove from the heat.

5 To serve, pack a small soup bowl to the brim with the rice and place a serving plate on top. Flip the plate and the bowl upside down, then remove the bowl so that you have a perfect mound of rice in the middle of the plate. Arrange the omelette strips, crispy shrimp, Chinese sausage, caramelised pork, sour mango, sliced shallots, snake beans and lime wedges around the rice. Sprinkle the rice with the chopped chillies and serve.

ROYAL FOOD

PAD PAK BUNG

Stir-fried water spinach

Pak bung, also known as water spinach or morning glory, is a leafy green vegetable commonly grown in Thailand, Vietnam, Cambodia and Malaysia. Used extensively in Thai soups, curries, stir-fries and side dishes, it has long, heart-shaped leaves and hollow stems, which have a deliciously crunchy texture. The most popular use for pak bung is in a dish called pad pak bung, which has entire street-food stalls in Bangkok dedicated to it. Pad pak bung involves stir-frying the vegetable over very high heat, with the highlight being the huge flame that erupts around the pan once the ingredients are added to the hot oil. It is a theatrical show for diners as much as it is a delicious culinary experience.

Serves 2

80 ml (2½ fl oz/⅓ cup) vegetable oil

5 garlic cloves, bruised with the flat blade of a knife

4 red bird's eye chillies, bruised with the flat blade of a knife

2 bunches water spinach, cut into 5 cm (2 in) pieces

1 tablespoon oyster sauce

1 tablespoon fermented soybean sauce (see glossary)

1 tablespoon soy sauce

1 teaspoon caster (superfine) sugar

steamed jasmine rice, to serve

1 Heat the oil in a wok over medium heat and sauté the garlic and chilli until fragrant. Increase the heat to high, add the water spinach and stir-fry for 2 minutes, until wilted. Season with the oyster sauce, fermented soybean sauce, soy sauce and caster sugar and stir-fry for a further minute.

2 Serve with steamed jasmine rice.

pad see eiw moo

Stir-fried rice noodles and pork with sweet soy sauce

Pad see eiw literally means 'stir-fried with soy sauce', and that is the essence of this immensely popular noodle dish. Like many of Thailand's national dishes, pad see eiw is a Chinese-influenced dish, and it is quite similar to the char kway teow of Malaysian and Singaporean cuisines. The type of noodles and meat used may differ, but the most common variation of the dish in Bangkok's street-food scene uses flat rice noodles and pork.

Serves 2

300 g (10½ oz) pork tenderloin, finely sliced

3 tablespoons dark soy sauce

300 g (10½ oz) fresh flat rice noodles

100 ml (3½ fl oz) vegetable oil

1 tablespoon crushed garlic

2 eggs, beaten

2 tablespoons fish sauce

2 tablespoons caster (superfine) sugar

1 tablespoon fermented soybean sauce (see glossary)

1 bunch Chinese broccoli (gai lan), finely sliced on the diagonal

pinch of ground white pepper

chilli flakes, to taste (optional)

Pork marinade

1 tablespoon crushed garlic

1 tablespoon caster (superfine) sugar

1 tablespoon tapioca flour

½ tablespoon fish sauce

1 teaspoon ground white pepper

1 tablespoon oyster sauce

1 tablespoon grapeseed oil

1 First, marinate the pork. Combine all the marinade ingredients in a large non-reactive bowl and add the sliced pork. Mix well, then cover with plastic wrap and transfer to the refrigerator to marinate for 1 hour.

2 In a separate bowl, mix the dark soy sauce and the flat noodles together, separating the noodles as you go. This will prevent the noodles from sticking to each other. Set aside.

3 Heat the oil in a wok over medium–high heat and stir-fry the garlic until fragrant. Add the marinated pork and stir-fry for 2–3 minutes. Pour in the beaten egg and stir with a spatula to roughly break it up, then push the egg to one side and leave to cook until golden.

4 Add the noodles, fish sauce, caster sugar and soybean sauce to the wok and stir-fry until the noodles are coated, taking care to stir continuously to prevent the noodles from sticking together. Add the Chinese broccoli and stir-fry until it softens, then taste the noodles and adjust the seasoning if necessary. Remove from the heat.

5 Divide the noodles between two plates and sprinkle with white pepper and chilli flakes, if desired, before serving.

Stir-fries

A wok and a frying pan are two of the most important cooking utensils in every Thai kitchen. Stir-frying over high heat, preferably on a gas stove, is very common in Thailand, with most Thai dishes involving stir-frying. Making curries requires curry pastes to be stir-fried to release their flavours; the famous noodle dishes pad thai and pad see eiw need to be stir-fried in very hot oil; and khao pad, or fried rice, is also the product of stir-frying – in fact, 'pad' means 'stir-fry'.

Chinese immigrants to Thailand introduced the technique of stir-frying in hot oil over a large flame centuries ago, and many of the stir-fried dishes in Thai cuisine are products of Chinese influence. Originally, dishes were stir-fried in earthenware pots, which were excellent at retaining heat. It wasn't until the fifteenth century that brass woks were introduced to Siam during the Ayutthaya period (1351–1767), thanks to trade with foreign merchants from places like Portugal. Aluminium and other metal equipment wasn't used until much later. Brass woks are still used in Thai kitchens today for certain dishes, especially desserts, because of the metal's ability to conduct even and stable heat.

When cooking stir-fried dishes, we highly recommend using a wok – and don't forget that high heat is the key to delicious stir-fries.

GAI YANG

Grilled chicken

Originally from northeast Thailand, gai yang has many different variations, though it is usually eaten with sticky rice and Papaya salad (page 99). There are a few very famous names who specialise in the classic grilled chicken dish – unsurprisingly, most are situated in the home of gai yang, northeastern Thailand. For Thai people, no gai yang is complete without dipping sauces, with the clear favourite being a tangy sauce made with toasted rice powder and tamarind juice.

Serves 4

1 whole 2 kg (4 lb 7 oz) chicken

7 coriander (cilantro) roots, scraped clean

3 lemongrass stalks

10 garlic cloves

1 tablespoon whole black peppercorns

2 red shallots

125 ml (4 fl oz/½ cup) evaporated milk

2 tablespoons oyster sauce

1 tablespoon soy sauce

1 teaspoon fine sea salt

2 pandan leaves

cooked sticky rice, to serve (optional)

Papaya salad (page 99), to serve (optional)

Dipping sauce

1–2 tablespoons fish sauce

2 tablespoons tamarind concentrate

1 tablespoon grated palm sugar

1–2 tablespoons lime juice

1 teaspoon toasted rice powder (see glossary)

1 teaspoon chilli flakes

1 tablespoon finely sliced spring onion (scallion)

coriander (cilantro) leaves, to garnish

1 First, butterfly the chicken. Place it breast-side down on a cutting board and, using a pair of kitchen scissors, cut along both sides of the backbone from the cavity to the neck. Remove the backbone and discard. Turn the chicken breast-side up and press firmly against the breastbone to break the bone and flatten the chicken. Place in a large container or non-reactive bowl and set aside.

2 Using a food processor, blend the coriander roots, lemongrass, garlic, black peppercorns, shallots and evaporated milk into a fine paste. Add the oyster sauce, soy sauce and salt, stirring to combine. Pour the mixture over the chicken, add the pandan leaves and mix well, making sure that all of the chicken is coated in the marinade. Set aside in the refrigerator to marinate for 30 minutes to 1 hour.

3 To make the dipping sauce, combine all of the ingredients except the spring onion and coriander in a small saucepan. Cook over low heat until the sugar dissolves, then remove from the heat and set aside to cool. Once cool, transfer to a small bowl and garnish with the spring onion and coriander.

4 Using a charcoal barbecue (grill), cook the chicken over low–medium heat until the internal temperature reaches 70°C (158°F) or the juices run clear (not pink) when a metal skewer is inserted into the thickest part of the thigh. Alternatively, if you don't have a charcoal barbecue, you can roast the chicken in a preheated 210°C (410°F) oven for 30 minutes, or until the chicken reaches temperature or passes the skewer test.

5 Serve the gai yang with the dipping sauce, accompanied with sticky rice and/or papaya salad, if desired.

NAM PRIK GAPI PLA TU

Fermented shrimp paste relish with deep-fried mackerel

Nam prik has been an important part of Thai cuisine since the fourteenth century, and is perhaps the oldest Thai sauce. Various herbs and spices are pounded in a mortar and pestle to create a purée, which is then flavoured with fish sauce, lime juice and tamarind paste, among other things. Nam prik is often served with vegetables or fish and is also used as a sauce for the rice-based stir-fry known as kao pad nam prik. The ingredients used to make nam prik vary from region to region, informed by the produce available to cooks. One of the essential ingredients in many variations of nam prik – and in this recipe – is gapi, a paste made from fermented shrimp.

Makes 1 cup

200 ml (7 fl oz) vegetable oil, for deep-frying

1 whole blue mackerel, cleaned

10 red and green bird's eye chillies, halved diagonally

10 garlic cloves

5 small red shallots, roughly chopped

pinch of fine sea salt

½ teaspoon caster (superfine) sugar

1 tablespoon fish sauce

1 tablespoon gapi (fermented shrimp paste; see glossary)

2 tablespoons lime juice

raw or blanched vegetables such as cucumber, Thai eggplants (aubergines), bamboo shoots, okra or green cabbage, to serve

steamed jasmine rice, to serve

1 Heat the oil in a wok or a deep heavy-based saucepan over medium heat until a cube of bread dropped into the oil browns in 30 seconds – approximately 180°C (350°F). Deep-fry the mackerel for 2–3 minutes until golden all over, then remove from the oil with a slotted spoon and transfer to paper towel to drain and cool. Once cool, remove all of the flesh, discarding the skin and bones, and set aside.

2 Toast the chilli, garlic and shallots in a dry wok over medium heat for 5–7 minutes, until soft and slightly charred. Transfer to a mortar and pestle and pound until smooth. Add the mackerel flesh and pound until smooth, then add the salt, caster sugar, fish sauce, gapi and lime juice and mix well. Add 2–3 tablespoons of warm water to adjust the consistency to your liking.

3 Serve the nam prik gapi pla tu with raw or blanched vegetables and steamed jasmine rice.

Rad na sen mi

Rice vermicelli in thick gravy

Rad na, a dish of noodles in thick gravy traditionally served in banana leaves, was brought to Thailand long ago by Chinese immigrants. Flat rice noodles and egg noodles are most often used in rad na, but sen mi, or rice vermicelli, are also common. Vital to a delicious rad na are high-quality noodles and, of course, a well-seasoned gravy. Cooked over high heat and caramelised with dark soy sauce, the noodles should be quite dry before being drenched in gravy, which usually contains fermented soybean sauce for a salty, full flavour. Rad na is widely available on the streets of Bangkok and is usually served with a side of chilli flakes and pickled chilli in white vinegar.

Serves 4

170 g (6 oz) dried rice vermicelli

80 ml (2½ fl oz/⅓ cup) vegetable oil

80 ml (2½ fl oz/⅓ cup) dark soy sauce

5 garlic cloves, finely chopped

500 g (1 lb 2 oz) banana prawns (shrimp), peeled

2 bunches Chinese broccoli (gai lan), finely sliced on the diagonal

1.5 litres (1½ quarts/6 cups) Pork stock (page 192)

1 tablespoon fermented soybean sauce (see glossary)

2 tablespoons soy sauce

2 tablespoons oyster sauce

1 teaspoon caster (superfine) sugar

75 g (2¾ oz) cornflour (corn starch)

ground white pepper, to serve

chilli flakes or pickled chillies, to serve

1 Fill a large bowl with cold water and soak the vermicelli until softened. Drain in a colander and set aside for 15 minutes to dry.

2 Heat 1 tablespoon of the oil in a wok over medium heat and stir-fry the vermicelli and dark soy sauce until the noodles are evenly coated. Transfer the noodles to a bowl and set aside.

3 Heat the remaining vegetable oil in a clean wok over medium heat and sauté the garlic until fragrant, then add the prawns and stir-fry until coloured all over. Add the Chinese broccoli and stir-fry for 2 minutes, until wilted, then pour in the stock. Bring to the boil and season with the fermented soybean sauce, soy sauce, oyster sauce and sugar.

4 In a small bowl, combine the cornflour and 60 ml (2 fl oz/¼ cup) water, stirring until smooth. Slowly drizzle the cornflour mixture into the wok, stirring constantly until the stock thickens.

5 To serve, divide the vermicelli among four plates and ladle over a generous amount of gravy. Arrange the prawns and Chinese broccoli on top. Season with pepper and chilli flakes or pickled chillies to taste.

Khao soi gai

Egg noodles in chicken curry

Khao soi came to Thailand with the Chinese Muslim immigrants who settled in northern Thailand, and has since become very popular in all parts of the country, including Bangkok. The dish combines coconut cream, gai (chicken), and herbs and spices to make a rich, warming dish suitable for the cold climate of the north. It is a must-eat menu item when visiting the northern parts of Thailand, especially in Chiang Mai, which is home to several famous khao sois.

Serves 2

500 ml (17 fl oz/2 cups) coconut cream

½ tablespoon curry powder

500 g (1 lb 2 oz) chicken drumsticks

1 tablespoon grated palm sugar

2 teaspoons fine sea salt

100 ml (3½ fl oz) vegetable oil

Egg noodles

250 g (9 oz) cake flour, plus extra for dusting

140 g (5 oz) beaten duck egg (about 4 eggs in total)

Curry paste

5 dried red chillies

5 garlic cloves

5 small red shallots

2 krachai (fingerroots; see glossary) or 5 thin slices galangal

1 teaspoon ground turmeric

1 tablespoon finely sliced lemongrass

1 tablespoon grated palm sugar

1½ tablespoons gapi (fermented shrimp paste; see glossary)

1 kaffir lime leaf, finely chopped

To serve

coriander (cilantro) leaves

finely sliced red shallots

lime wedges

pickled mustard greens (see glossary)

1 First, make the egg noodles. Sift the flour through a mesh sieve into a mixing bowl. Make a well in the centre of the flour and pour in the beaten egg. Use a fork to gradually incorporate the flour until a dough is formed. Knead the dough with your hands for 10 minutes, or until the dough is smooth. Wrap the dough in a clean, damp kitchen towel and set aside to rest for a minimum of 30 minutes.

2 Lightly dust your work surgace with flour, divide the dough into four pieces and prepare your pasta machine. Working with one piece of dough at a time, keeping the remaining dough covered with the damp kitchen towel, flatten the dough into a disc and feed it through the machine set to its widest setting. Fold the dough into thirds and feed it through the machine again. Repeat the process with the machine set to the next widest setting, dusting with flour as needed, until you have rolled out the dough into a sheet roughly 1 mm (1⁄32 in) thick. Cut into 2 mm (1⁄16 in) wide noodles, twist into a loose pile and set aside. Repeat with the remaining dough pieces.

3 To make the curry paste, combine all the ingredients in a mortar and pestle and pound into a fine paste. Set aside.

4 In a large saucepan, heat half the coconut cream over medium heat until it is almost boiling. Add the curry paste and sauté until fragrant. Add the curry powder, stirring to combine, followed by the chicken. Stir to coat the chicken and add the remaining coconut cream, along with the palm sugar and salt. Cover with a lid, reduce the heat to very low and simmer for 40 minutes.

5 In a wok or a large heavy-based frying pan, heat the oil over high heat and fry a small handful of the egg noodles until golden brown and crisp. Remove from the oil with a slotted spoon and set aside on paper towel to drain.

6 Fill a large bowl with iced water and set aside. Bring a saucepan of water to the boil over high heat and blanch the remaining egg noodles for 1–2 minutes, until al dente. Using tongs, transfer the noodles to the iced water to shock, then to a colander to drain.

7 To serve, divide the egg noodles between two bowls and ladle the curry over the top. Garnish with coriander, shallots, lime wedges, pickled mustard greens and the fried noodles.

Salads

Thai salads, or yum, are versatile dishes of meat or seafood tossed with fresh herbs and typically dressed with chilli, lime juice and fish sauce. Mint, coriander, Thai basil, lemongrass, kaffir lime leaves and red shallots are some of the principal herbs and aromatics, while certain types of yum also contain coconut cream and nam prik pao (Thai chilli paste) to add richness and heat. There are many different takes on the dish and your imagination is the only limit when it comes to selecting ingredients. However, there are two critical factors to making a good yum: the balance and layering of the flavours, which can sometimes be difficult to achieve, and the freshness of the ingredients.

Northeastern Thailand has its own style of yum, the popular dish known as laap. This salad contains slightly different herbs, as well as the addition of ground toasted rice. Along with another famous yum from the northeast, som tum (papaya salad), laap is influenced by the cuisine of neighbouring Laos. Glutinous rice is essential to accompany laap and som tum when eaten in the northeastern part of the country, another Laotian influence.

Bangkok is full of restaurants and street-food stalls dedicated to the art of yum. Street vendors selling yum can be identified by their stainless-steel mixing bowls and displays of herbs and other fresh ingredients, but what each stall specialises in is the kind of knowledge only a local has. Restaurants usually offer superior salad menus with higher quality ingredients compared to those available on the streets. With their fresh ingredients and pungent flavours, yum are some of the most popular dishes in Thailand, and can be eaten on their own, with steamed rice or with khao tom (rice soup) if served for a late-night supper.

YUM RUAM MID TALAY

Mixed seafood salad

Yum (salad) is a very popular option for anyone wanting a light, healthy meal, and there are dedicated street-food stalls around Bangkok specialising in various versions. It is simple to cook and is one of Thai cuisine's most versatile dishes, with ingredients varying according to diner (or chef) preference. The most important component of the dish is the dressing, which unifies all of the ingredients with the flavours of fresh lime juice, chilli and garlic.

Serves 2

2 tablespoons fine sea salt

50 g (1¾ oz) barramundi fillet or other white fish fillet, cut into bite-sized pieces

50 g (1¾ oz) tiger prawns (shrimp), peeled and deveined, tails intact

50 g (1¾ oz) squid, cleaned and sliced into rings

10 mussels, cleaned and debearded

½ onion, finely sliced

1 tomato, diced

1 Chinese celery stalk (see glossary), cut into 2–3 cm (¾–1¼ in) pieces

Dressing

2 tablespoons fish sauce

2 tablespoons lime juice

1½ teaspoons caster (superfine) sugar

1 tablespoon sliced red bird's eye chilli

1 small red shallot, very finely sliced

2 garlic cloves, finely chopped

1 Half-fill a saucepan with water, add the salt and bring to a rolling boil over high heat. Poach the barramundi in the salted water for 3 minutes, then remove with a slotted spoon and set aside to drain. Poach the prawns and squid for 1–2 minutes, then remove with a slotted spoon and set aside to drain. Remove all but 250 ml (8½ fl oz/1 cup) water from the saucepan, bring back to the boil, add the mussels and cover with the lid. Reduce the heat to medium and steam, stirring occasionally, until the mussels open wide. Remove the mussels from their shells, discarding any unopened mussels, and set aside.

2 To make the dressing, combine all the ingredients in a small bowl and stir until the sugar dissolves.

3 Combine the cooked seafood, onion, tomato, Chinese celery and dressing in a large bowl and mix gently until well coated. Serve at room temperature.

YUM SOM OH

Pomelo salad

Yum som oh is originally from the north of Thailand, where it is sometimes prepared in a similar way to Papaya salad (page 99). Pomelo's crisp texture and sweet and sour flavour have made it a fruit much loved by the Thai people; it is also eaten on its own with a condiment made of sugar, salt and chilli flakes.

Serves 2–3

350 g (12¼ oz) tiger prawns (shrimp), peeled and deveined, tails intact

100 g (3½ oz) minced (ground) pork

100 ml (3½ fl oz) vegetable oil, for frying

2 red shallots, finely sliced

1 small pomelo, peeled, segments torn into pieces

2 tablespoons roasted peanuts, crushed

50 g (1¾ oz) dried shrimp (see glossary), pounded

2 tablespoons desiccated (shredded) coconut

1 tablespoon chilli flakes

2 tablespoons lime juice

chopped coriander (cilantro) leaves or betel leaves, to garnish

Dressing

80 ml (2½ fl oz/⅓ cup) coconut cream

4 teaspoons grated palm sugar

2 tablespoons fish sauce

2 tablespoons tamarind concentrate

1 tablespoon nam prik pao (Thai chilli paste; see glossary)

1 Fill a small saucepan with water and bring to a rolling boil over high heat. Poach the prawns for 1–2 minutes, until coloured, then remove using a slotted spoon and set aside. Repeat the process with the pork, increasing the cooking time to 2–3 minutes, until no more pink remains.

2 Next, make the dressing. In a small saucepan over medium heat, bring the coconut cream just to the boil, then remove from the heat and set aside to cool to room temperature. In a separate saucepan, combine the palm sugar, fish sauce, tamarind concentrate, nam prik pao and 1 tablespoon water and cook over low heat until the sugar dissolves. Add the coconut cream and mix well. Remove from the heat and set aside to cool.

3 Heat the oil in a small saucepan over medium heat until it shimmers. Add the shallots and fry until golden and crisp. Remove from the oil with a slotted spoon and set aside to drain on paper towel.

4 In a large bowl, combine the pomelo, peanuts, dried shrimp, fried shallots, desiccated coconut, chilli flakes and lime juice. Slowly drizzle in the dressing while gently mixing; the pomelo will release juice as you mix, so be a little conservative with the dressing to prevent the salad from getting too wet. Add the cooked prawns and pork and stir gently, adding a little more dressing if the salad is too dry at this point. Serve sprinkled with coriander or with betel leaves on the side.

Clockwise from top: Minced chicken salad (page 97);
Glass noodle salad (page 96); Mixed seafood salad (page 92).

yum woonsen

Glass noodle salad

Yum woonsen is another type of yum, or salad, that is highly popular among Thai people. There are many variations on yum woonsen, with the most common ones featuring minced (ground) pork or seafood. Some street food vendors use wood ear fungus, which makes for a great vegetarian take on this salad.

Serves 4

250 g (9 oz) dried glass noodles

3 tablespoons vegetable oil, for frying

4 garlic cloves, finely chopped

25 g (1 oz) dried shrimp (see glossary)

100 g (3½ oz) minced (ground) pork

3½ tablespoons fish sauce

¼ red onion, finely sliced

3½ tablespoons lime juice

1½ teaspoons caster (superfine) sugar

2 tablespoons sliced red bird's eye chillies

small handful roughly chopped coriander (cilantro) leaves and stalks

small handful roughly chopped spring onion (scallion)

25 g (1 oz) roasted peanuts

1 Fill a large bowl with cold water and soak the glass noodles until softened. Drain in a colander and fill the bowl with iced water. Bring a saucepan of water to the boil over high heat and blanch the noodles for 10–20 seconds. Using tongs, transfer the noodles to the iced water to shock. Once cool, drain in a colander and set aside.

2 Heat the oil in a non-stick frying pan over medium heat and sauté the garlic for 4–5 minutes, until golden. Remove from the oil with a slotted spoon and set aside to drain on paper towel. Fry the dried shrimp in the same oil for 2–3 minutes, until crisp. Remove from the oil and set aside to drain on paper towel. Reserve the oil and allow to cool to room temperature.

3 Bring a small saucepan of water to the boil over high heat and cook the pork, stirring constantly to break it apart, for 2–3 minutes, until no more pink remains. Drain most of the water off, return the saucepan to the stove and reduce the heat to medium. Add 1 tablespoon of fish sauce and sauté the pork for 2 minutes, then remove from the heat and set aside to cool.

4 Combine the noodles, fried garlic, reserved oil, fried shrimp, red onion and pork mince in a large non-reactive bowl and mix well. Season with the remaining fish sauce, lime juice, caster sugar and chillies, adjusting the balance of flavours to your liking, if necessary.

5 Transfer to a serving plate and garnish with coriander, spring onion and toasted peanuts.

Laap gai

Minced chicken salad

Laap, a classic dish from the northern and northeastern parts of Thailand, is thought to have come from the south of China, arriving with merchants long ago. Originally made in a similar way to steak tartare, with raw meat tossed with herbs and spices, laap is today more commonly made with cooked meat. The salad has many regional variations, but the essential ingredients are always red shallots, sawtooth coriander and ground toasted rice. Laap is usually accompanied with a side of raw herbs and vegetables such as mint, cabbage and green beans.

Serves 2

300 g (10½ oz) minced (ground) chicken

2 tablespoons jasmine rice

1 tablespoon chilli flakes

3 tablespoons fish sauce

3 tablespoons lime juice

4 small red shallots, finely sliced

1 spring onion (scallion), finely sliced

7 g (¼ oz/⅓ cup) peppermint leaves, roughly chopped

1 sawtooth coriander leaf, finely sliced

1 Bring 125 ml (4 fl oz/½ cup) water to the boil in a small saucepan over high heat and cook the chicken, stirring constantly to break it apart, for 2–3 minutes, until no more pink remains. Drain and set aside to cool.

2 In a dry frying pan over medium heat, toast the jasmine rice until it turns a dark golden brown. Using a spice grinder or mortar and pestle, grind or pound the rice into a fine powder.

3 Combine the chilli flakes, fish sauce, lime juice, ground toasted rice, shallots, spring onion, peppermint, sawtooth coriander and chicken in a large non-reactive bowl. Mix well before serving.

SOM TUM THAI

Papaya salad

Hailing from the northeastern part of Thailand, som tum has been embraced as a national dish, to the extent that songs have been written in tribute to this much-loved salad. 'Som' means 'sour' in the dialect of Thai spoken in the northeast, and 'tum' is a method of mixing ingredients using a mortar and pestle. There are many variations on and additions to the dish: pla ra (fermented fish sauce) is sometimes used for a more complex flavour, while boo kem (salted crab) is often added by those who want a saltier hit. Som tum thai is a sweeter and milder version that includes roasted peanuts.

Serves 2

1 tablespoon dried shrimp (see glossary)

2 garlic cloves

4–5 red bird's eye chillies

50 g (1¾ oz) snake (yard-long) beans, cut into 5 cm (2 in) lengths

½ tablespoon roasted peanuts

20 g (¾ oz) palm sugar, melted (see Chef's notes, page 10)

2 tablespoons fish sauce

1 tablespoon lime juice

5 cherry tomatoes, halved

200 g (7 oz) green papaya, peeled and julienned

cooked sticky rice, to serve (optional)

Grilled chicken (page 80), to serve (optional)

1 Using a large mortar and pestle, coarsely pound the dried shrimp until they start to break apart. Add the garlic cloves and chillies and pound them into a coarse paste, then add the snake beans and peanuts, pounding them until the peanuts have been roughly broken up.

2 Mix in the palm sugar using the pestle and stir until the sugar dissolves. Add the fish sauce, lime juice and cherry tomatoes and use both a pounding and stirring action to combine. Finally, add the green papaya, stirring and gently pounding all the ingredients to mix well.

3 Check the som tum for seasoning; it should taste sweet, sour, salty and spicy. Adjust the seasoning if necessary and serve with warm sticky rice and grilled chicken, if desired.

KHAO MUN GAI

Hainanese chicken rice

Originally from Hainan in China, Hainanese chicken rice may seem like a strange recipe to include in this book. But this well-known dish has travelled with Hainanese migrants throughout Southeast Asia, and is widely available on the streets of Bangkok, where vendors hang whole cooked chickens in their shop windows to signify their specialty. The highlight of the dish is the fragrant rice cooked in chicken broth with ginger and garlic, which is served with slow-poached chicken and a dipping sauce on the side that adds sweetness and sourness to the dish. There are a few creative versions of khao mun gai in Bangkok, with grilled chicken and fried chicken options becoming very popular among locals.

Serves 6

1 whole ginger root, sliced on the diagonal

1 Chinese cabbage (wombok), roughly chopped

5 coriander (cilantro) roots, scraped clean

20 whole white peppercorns

2 tablespoons soy sauce

2 pandan leaves, tied into a knot

1 × 2.5–3 kg (5 lb 8 oz–6 lb 10 oz) free-range chicken

3 tablespoons fine sea salt

3 tablespoons caster (superfine) sugar

Rice

500 g (1 lb 2 oz) chicken skin, roughly chopped

1 red shallot, finely sliced

30 g (1 oz) garlic cloves, roughly chopped

1 × 5 cm (2 in) piece ginger, sliced on the diagonal

400 g (14 oz) jasmine rice

1 teaspoon fine sea salt

1 teaspoon caster (superfine) sugar

1 pandan leaf, tied into a knot

Dipping sauce

1 tablespoon fermented soybean sauce (see glossary)

2½ tablespoons soy sauce

1½ tablespoons sweet soy sauce

80 g (2¾ oz) young ginger, grated

1½ tablespoons white vinegar

juice of ½ lime

2 tablespoons chopped red and green bird's eye chillies

1 Bring 6 litres (6 quarts) water to the boil in a large stockpot over high heat and add the ginger, Chinese cabbage, coriander roots, whole white peppercorns, soy sauce and pandan leaves. Carefully lower the chicken into the pot and reduce the heat to low–medium. Add the salt and caster sugar and simmer for approximately 45 minutes, until the chicken is cooked through.

2 Fill a large bowl with iced water and remove the stockpot from the heat. Using a pair of tongs, transfer the chicken to the iced water. Once cool, drain the chicken and remove any excess moisture with paper towel. With a ladle or a large spoon, scoop out as much of the chicken fat on the surface of the stock as possible. Rub the chicken skin with a little of the fat to prevent it from drying out and reserve the remaining fat, as well as the chicken stock.

3 To make the rice, slowly render the chicken skin in a wok over medium heat for 30–40 minutes, stirring occasionally and reducing the heat if it darkens too quickly, until the skin is golden brown and the fat has rendered out. Remove the skin with a slotted spoon and set aside to drain on paper towel (this crispy skin can be used to garnish other dishes). Add the shallot to the chicken skin oil and sauté for 4–5 minutes. Strain the oil through a mesh sieve into a bowl and discard the shallot.

4 In a clean wok, heat 80 ml (2½ fl oz/⅓ cup) of the chicken skin oil over medium heat and stir-fry the garlic and ginger until fragrant. Add the rice and stir to coat with the oil, then pour in 30 g (1 oz) of the reserved chicken fat from the stock, along with the salt and caster sugar. Add 250 ml (8½ fl oz/1 cup) of the reserved chicken stock and stir-fry until the rice grains turn a cloudy white. Remove from the heat.

5 Place the pandan leaf in the bowl of a rice cooker (see note) and cover with the rice. Add enough chicken stock to cover the rice by about 2 cm (¾ in) and cook according to manufacturer instructions. Once cooked, leave on the 'keep warm' setting for 15–20 minutes before opening the lid to remove the ginger and the pandan leaf. Stir with a paddle to thoroughly mix and transfer to a serving plate.

6 Meanwhile, make the dipping sauce by combining all the ingredients except the chillies in a small bowl. Add 1½ tablespoons water, mix well and check the seasoning; adjust the amount of sweetness and sourness to your liking. Add the chopped chilli to taste just before serving.

7 Dilute the remaining chicken stock with water to taste, bring to the boil and ladle into six small soup bowls. Carve the chicken into 1 cm (½ in) slices and arrange over the top of the rice. Serve accompanied with the dipping sauce and bowls of stock.

Note

We recommend using a rice cooker to make this dish, as it is simple and produces the best results. Cooking it in a saucepan is more likely to lead to burned rice, but it can be done. Use a 1:1 ratio of liquid to rice. Cover and bring to the boil over high heat, then immediately reduce the heat to very low. Allow the rice to cook, covered, until it is tender, checking periodically to make sure the rice is not burning on the bottom. Remove from the heat and allow to rest without removing the lid for 15–20 minutes before serving.

KHaO MHOK GaI

Yellow rice with chicken

When merchants from India and the Middle East visited Thailand in the nineteenth century, they brought with them biryani, a dish of spiced meat and rice. This Thai take on biryani pairs chicken marinated in a complex blend of spices with buttery rice and a sweet-sour dipping sauce. Although khao mhok gai did not originate in Thailand, it has long been considered part of Thai cuisine, and is widely available in Bangkok and in the south of the country, especially among the region's Muslim communities.

Serves 8

8 chicken leg quarters or drumsticks

55 g (2 oz) unsalted butter

500 g (1 lb 2 oz) jasmine rice

1 litre (1 quart/4 cups) Chicken stock (page 193)

coriander (cilantro) leaves, to garnish

20 g (¾ oz/¼ cup) fried shallots

sliced cucumber, tomato and lettuce, to serve

Marinade

2 cinnamon sticks

6 green cardamom pods

6 cloves

2 teaspoons ground coriander

1 tablespoon whole white peppercorns

5 garlic cloves, roughly chopped

1 × 2 cm (¾ in) piece ginger, chopped

2 red chillies, deseeded

½ teaspoon chilli flakes

2 teaspoons fine sea salt

2 teaspoons curry powder

1 teaspoon ground turmeric

1 teaspoon ground cumin

150 g (5½ oz) natural yoghurt

60 ml (2 fl oz/¼ cup) evaporated milk

Dipping sauce

100 g (3½ oz) caster (superfine) sugar

2 teaspoons fine sea salt

4 spring onions (scallions), roughly chopped

5 coriander sprigs, roughly chopped

1 whole small ginger root, finely chopped

2 green bird's eye chillies, roughly chopped

10 garlic cloves

10 g (¼ oz/½ cup) peppermint leaves

125 ml (4½ fl oz/½ cup) white vinegar

1 First, prepare the marinade. In a frying pan or wok over medium heat, toast the cinnamon sticks, cardamom pods, cloves, ground coriander and white peppercorns until fragrant. Using a mortar and pestle, pound the spices into a fine powder and set aside. Pound the garlic, ginger and red chillies into a fine paste, then add the toasted spices. Transfer to a large non-reactive bowl or container and stir in the remaining ingredients until well incorporated.

2 Poke the chicken pieces all over with a fork and place in the marinade, mixing well to ensure all pieces are evenly coated. Cover, transfer to the refrigerator and leave to marinate for a minimum of 1 hour or, preferably, overnight.

3 Meanwhile, make the dipping sauce. Heat the caster sugar, salt and 80 ml (2½ fl oz/⅓ cup) water in a small saucepan over low heat until the sugar dissolves. Remove from the heat and set aside to cool. In a food processor, blend the spring onion, coriander, ginger, chilli, garlic and peppermint into a paste. Stir the vinegar into the cooled syrup, followed by the paste. Mix well to combine and set aside.

4 In a wok or large heavy-based frying pan, melt the butter over medium heat. Remove the chicken pieces from the marinade, reserving the marinade, and fry until golden brown all over. Transfer to a plate and set aside. Add the rice and the chicken marinade to the wok and stir to combine. Remove from the heat and transfer to the bowl of a rice cooker (see note).

5 Nestle the chicken pieces in the rice and add enough chicken stock to cover the rice by 2 cm (¾ in). Cook according to manufacturer instructions; once cooked, leave on the 'keep warm' setting for 15 minutes before opening the lid.

6 Transfer the chicken rice to a serving plate and garnish with the coriander and shallots. Serve with the cucumber, tomato and lettuce and the dipping sauce.

Note

If you don't have a rice cooker, or if your rice cooker is not large enough, place the rice and chicken in a wide, deep saucepan and add 750 ml (25½ fl oz/3 cups) of the stock. Cover and bring to the boil over high heat, then immediately reduce the heat to low. Cook, covered, until the rice is tender and the chicken is cooked through, checking periodically to make sure the rice is not burning on the bottom. Remove from the heat and allow to rest without removing the lid for 15–20 minutes before serving.

Khai palo

Egg and pork in sweet soy broth

Khai palo is a real favourite among Bangkok locals, and it can typically be found at almost every market and ready-to-eat hawker stand in the city. Like many other Thai dishes, khai palo was introduced to Thailand by Chinese immigrants – its soy sauce broth sweetened by dark brown sugar and flavoured with cinnamon and star anise will taste familiar to Chinese-food enthusiasts. Pork belly, the traditional protein, provides a rich, umami flavour to the soup, but khai palo with chicken or duck can also be found. It is sweet, savoury and best eaten with rice.

Serves 3

6 duck eggs

2 tablespoons grapeseed oil

1½ tablespoons Three-spice paste (page 194)

100 g (3½ oz) palm sugar, grated

150 g (5½ oz) pork belly, cut into 1 cm (½ in) thick slices

250 g (9 oz) firm tofu, cut into cubes

1 tablespoon sweet soy sauce

1 tablespoon soy sauce

2 teaspoons fine sea salt

2 cinnamon sticks

4 star anise

coriander (cilantro) leaves, to garnish

steamed jasmine rice, to serve (optional)

1 Fill a large bowl with iced water and set aside. Bring a saucepan of water to the boil over high heat and boil the eggs for 6 minutes. Using a slotted spoon, transfer the eggs to the iced water. Once the eggs are cool, peel them and set aside.

2 Heat the oil in a large saucepan over medium heat and sauté the three-spice paste until fragrant. Add the palm sugar and cook until it caramelises and turns a dark golden brown, stirring constantly to avoid burning. Once the sugar is caramelised, add the sliced pork belly and tofu. Stir-fry for 2 minutes, then add the boiled eggs and stir gently for a further minute, taking care not to break the eggs.

3 Add 1.2 litres (1.2 quarts) of water to the saucepan, along with the sweet soy sauce, soy sauce, salt, cinnamon and star anise, and bring to the boil. Reduce the heat to low and simmer for 1 hour, skimming off any impurities that rise to the surface.

4 Remove from the heat and check the seasoning, adding more salt to taste if necessary. Ladle into soup bowls and garnish with the coriander leaves. Serve with steamed jasmine rice, if desired.

Mid

GAENG JUET MARA YAD SAI

Stuffed bitter melon soup

There are two types of mara, or bitter melon, in Thailand: mara khi knok, which is small, oval in shape, and rarely available outside Thailand; and Chinese mara, which is larger, light green and much more common. As the name suggests, bitter melon has a bitter flavour, but it's considered to have many health benefits; the bitterness can be reduced by rubbing the vegetable with salt. Mara features in several Thai dishes, with this soup being a popular choice at takeaway food vendors and late-night supper hawkers.

Serves 2

2 bitter melons

1 tablespoon fine sea salt

1 litre (1 quart/4 cups) Pork stock (page 192)

1 coriander (cilantro) root, scraped clean and bruised with the flat blade of a knife

3 shiitake mushrooms, cut into thirds

2 tablespoons soy sauce

1 teaspoon oyster sauce

½ teaspoon ground white pepper

½ teaspoon caster (superfine) sugar

coriander (cilantro) leaves, to garnish

Pork stuffing

50 g (1¾ oz) dried glass noodles

½ teaspoon caster (superfine) sugar

1 teaspoon fish sauce

1 teaspoon oyster sauce

1 tablespoon soy sauce

1 teaspoon chopped coriander (cilantro) root

1 teaspoon chopped garlic

½ teaspoon ground white pepper

200 g (7 oz) minced (ground) pork

1 Cut the bitter melons crossways into 5–6 cm (2–2¼ in) pieces and scoop out the seeds and white flesh. In a small bowl, combine the sea salt with enough water to make a paste, then rub the bitter melon pieces all over with the salt paste and set aside to rest for 15 minutes. This will reduce the bitter flavour of the bitter melon.

2 Meanwhile, prepare the pork stuffing. Fill a bowl with cold water and soak the glass noodles until softened. Drain in a colander and set aside. In a large mixing bowl, combine all the remaining ingredients except the pork and mix well. Add the pork and the glass noodles and knead until the sauce is incorporated. Gather the stuffing mixture into a ball and throw it into the bottom of the bowl so that it makes a loud slapping noise. Repeat the slapping process until the mixture becomes smoother and firmer, then set aside.

3 Fill a large bowl with iced water and set aside. Rinse the bitter melon pieces and place in a saucepan. Cover with water, bring to the boil over high heat and cook for 1 minute. Using a slotted spoon, transfer the bitter melon to the iced water to shock. Once cool, drain in a colander and pat dry with paper towel.

4 Stuff the bitter melon pieces with the pork stuffing, packing it tightly between the top and bottom rims of each piece.

5 Bring the pork stock to the boil in a large saucepan over medium heat. Add the coriander root, shiitake mushrooms and stuffed bitter melon. Bring to the boil again and season with the soy sauce, oyster sauce, white pepper and caster sugar. Stir gently to combine, reduce the heat to low, cover with a lid and simmer for 1 hour.

6 To serve, divide the soup between two bowls and scatter with coriander to garnish.

GAENG SOM PAK GOONG SOD

Sour orange curry with prawns and mixed vegetables

Gaeng som is one of the most interesting dishes to try when travelling in Thailand, as each region has its own variation. In the south, turmeric is added; in the west, fresh chilli and holy basil; while in the east kaffir lime leaves are used to create the sour flavour. This recipe is for the gaeng som that you'll find in Bangkok, which gets its sourness from tamarind concentrate. Fish and prawn (shrimp) are the usual proteins, while vegetables might include green papaya, snake (yard-long) beans, okra and water spinach, though they can be substituted for any vegetable you have on hand. If you're in a hurry, you can substitute two tablespoons of ready-made sour curry paste for the homemade version in this recipe, but making your own is worth the effort.

Serves 4

750 ml (25½ fl oz/3 cups) Chicken stock (page 193) or water

150 g (5½ oz) barramundi fillet, finely sliced

125 ml (4 fl oz/½ cup) tamarind concentrate

1 tablespoon grated palm sugar

3 tablespoons fish sauce

300 g (10½ oz) banana prawns (shrimp), peeled and deveined

mixed vegetables, such as snake (yard-long) beans, Chinese cabbage (wombok), white asparagus and okra (see note)

steamed jasmine rice, to serve

Sour curry paste

8 small red shallots, finely chopped

1 tablespoon finely chopped galangal

2 tablespoons chilli flakes

1¼ tablespoons gapi (fermented shrimp paste; see glossary)

large pinch of fine sea salt

1 First, make the curry paste. Combine all the ingredients in a mortar and pestle and pound into a fine paste.

2 Bring the stock to the boil in a large saucepan over high heat. Add the curry paste and stir until combined. Add the barramundi, allow to return to the boil and season with tamarind concentrate, palm sugar and fish sauce.

3 Add the prawns and cook, without stirring, for 3–5 minutes (it's important not to stir, as the stock will have an overwhelming seafood taste otherwise). Add the vegetables and cook until tender; if using cabbage or leafy greens, add them once the other vegetables are cooked. Check for seasoning – the curry should be sour, salty and spicy – and serve with steamed jasmine rice.

Mid

111

Note

The amount of vegetables used in this curry depends on your personal preference, so you can make it as vegetable-heavy as you like. However, we recommend that you don't overcrowd the broth.

Khanom Mor Gaeng

Taro custard with fried shallots

Khanom mor gaeng, also known as khanom gumpamat, was introduced to Thai cuisine during the reign of King Narai in the seventeenth century. Originally served to the royal court in a brass pot (the literal translation of the name is 'a dessert made in a curry pot'), these days khanom mor gaeng is baked and served in small square stainless-steel moulds. Phetchaburi, a province in the southwest of Thailand, is well known for its khanom mor gaeng; here the traditional method of cooking the dessert involves slowly baking and smoking it with burnt coconut husks, resulting in a very smooth custard. Mung beans or lotus seeds are common substitutes for the taro, and the topping of fried shallots is a must – even though it may seem unusual!

Serves 6

200 g (7 oz) taro, peeled and diced

80 ml (2½ fl oz/⅓ cup) vegetable oil

50 g (1¾ oz) red shallots, very finely sliced

5 duck eggs, beaten

4 pandan leaves

250 g (9 oz/⅔ cup lightly packed) coconut sugar

400 ml (13½ fl oz) coconut cream

1 Preheat the oven to 100°C (230°F).

2 Bring a large saucepan of water to the boil over high heat. Place the taro in the bottom of a large bamboo steamer and steam for 15 minutes, until soft. Purée the taro in a food processor and set aside.

3 Heat the oil in a small saucepan over medium heat until it shimmers. Add the shallots and fry until golden and crisp. Remove from the oil with a slotted spoon and set aside to drain on paper towel.

4 Combine the egg and pandan leaves in a large bowl. Squeeze the pandan leaves with your hands to infuse the eggs with the pandan aroma. Add the coconut sugar and coconut cream and mix well to combine.

5 Squeeze the pandan leaves once more, then strain the mixture into another large bowl to remove the leaves and any lumps. Stir in the taro purée until smooth and well incorporated.

6 Divide the custard mix between six 11 cm (4¼ in) square moulds or similarly sized ramekins and bake for 50 minutes, until set. Before serving, sprinkle with the fried shallots.

Khanom tan

Toddy palm cake

Khanom tan is thought to have originated in the thirteenth century, during the Sukhothai period (1238–1438), when it was made with rice flour, palm sugar and coconut. More common in Thai provinces that grow toddy palm or sugar palm trees, khanom tan has a soft texture and a sweet, creamy aroma. It is traditionally steamed in banana leaves, which adds further sweet notes to the cake. Due to a decrease in the number of toddy palm trees and fruit in Thailand, khanom tan is becoming rarer, and great versions of the cake are no longer easily found. If toddy palm purée is unavailable, it can be substituted with sweet potato or pumpkin purée. Take care to use very fine rice flour to ensure the cake has a smooth texture once steamed.

Serves 10

375 ml (12½ fl oz/1½ cups) coconut cream

150 g (7 oz) caster (superfine) sugar

4 pandan leaves

175 g (6 oz) cooked toddy palm purée (see glossay), or sweet potato or pumpkin purée (see note)

250 g (9 oz) rice flour

1 tablespoon baking powder

90 g (3 oz/1 cup loosely packed) fresh young coconut meat, shredded

1 Warm the coconut cream in a small saucepan over low heat. Add the caster sugar and stir until dissolved, then remove from the heat. Add the pandan leaves to the sweetened coconut cream and, when the mixture is cool enough to handle, squeeze them until they become soft. Discard the pandan leaves.

2 Transfer the coconut cream to a large mixing bowl and whisk in the toddy palm purée until smooth and well incorporated. Add the flour and baking powder and whisk to combine. Cover and set aside to rest at room temperature for 1 hour.

3 Bring a large saucepan of water to the boil over high heat. Divide the batter between ten 6.5 cm (2½ in) ramekins and place them in the bottom of a large bamboo steamer. Top each ramekin with a little of the shredded coconut meat and steam the cakes for 20–25 minutes, until risen and a skewer inserted into the centre of a cake comes out clean.

4 Remove from the heat and allow to cool before serving.

Note

To make sweet potato or pumpkin purée, bring a large saucepan of water to the boil over high heat. Place 175 g (6 oz) peeled and diced sweet potato or pumpkin in the bottom of a large bamboo steamer and steam for 15 minutes, until soft. Purée the sweet potato or pumpkin in a food processor.

KHANOM TUAY
Coconut milk custard

Khanom tuay is an ancient Thai dessert that is fortunately not too difficult to find in Bangkok's markets. Two layers of custard are steamed in a kind of ramekin called a talai. The bottom layer of the custard is creamy and sweet, whereas the top layer is made of salted coconut cream for contrast. Talai are usually 2.5 cm (1 in) deep and 6.5 cm (2½ in) in diameter; any similarly sized ramekins can be substituted.

Serves 5

5 pandan leaves, chopped

65 g (2¼ oz) rice flour

3 tablespoons arrowroot flour

120 g (4 oz) grated palm sugar or coconut sugar

250 ml (8½ fl oz/1 cup) coconut milk

Topping

500 ml (17 fl oz/2 cups) coconut cream

35 g (1¼ oz) rice flour

1 teaspoon fine sea salt

1 Using a food processor, blend the pandan leaves and 100 ml (3½ fl oz) water until the water turns green and the pandan leaves are all crushed. Squeeze the bruised pandan leaves to extract all of the water, strain the liquid through a mesh sieve into a large mixing bowl and discard the leaves.

2 Add the flours and palm sugar to the pandan water and use your hand to mix until the sugar dissolves and the custard mixture is smooth. Stir in the coconut milk and strain through a mesh sieve into another bowl to remove any lumps from the custard. Set aside.

3 To make the topping, combine all the ingredients in a bowl and strain through a mesh sieve into another bowl to remove any sediment. Set aside.

4 Bring a large saucepan of water to the boil over high heat. Fill five 60 ml (2 fl oz) capacity ramekins halfway with the custard mixture and place them in the bottom of a large bamboo steamer. Steam for 8 minutes, until firm.

5 Divide the topping mixture among the ramekins and continue to steam for a further 10 minutes, keeping the heat high to ensure a custard with a smooth consistency.

6 Remove from the heat and allow to cool before serving.

KHAO NIAEW NA GOONG

Sweet yellow sticky rice with sweetened prawns

Rice and glutinous rice are at the heart of Thai cuisine, and are used in both savoury and sweet dishes. In fact, many Thai desserts combine sweet with savoury. Khao niaew na goong is one such dish, and is one of the most-loved desserts in Thailand. Glutinous rice is cooked and flavoured with coconut, then served with a spiced, sweetened prawn (shrimp) topping. Dried shrimp can be used for this recipe, but fresh prawns are best for their flavour and texture. Khao niaew na goong is served at room temperature.

Serves 6

300 g (15½ oz) uncooked white glutinous rice, soaked overnight in cold water, or 500 g (1 lb 2 oz) cooked white glutinous rice

200 ml (7 fl oz) coconut milk

100 g (3½ oz) caster (superfine) sugar

1 teaspoon fine sea salt

1 tablespoon ground turmeric

Sweetened prawns

½ teaspoon whole white peppercorns

4 coriander (cilantro) roots, scraped clean

8 garlic cloves

3 tablespoons vegetable oil, for frying

5 kaffir lime leaves, finely chopped

200 g (7 oz) banana prawns (shrimp), peeled, deveined and minced

150 g (5½ oz) caster (superfine) sugar

½ teaspoon fine sea salt

250 g (9 oz) unsweetened shredded coconut

1 drop orange food colouring (optional)

200 ml (7 fl oz) coconut cream

1 Fill a saucepan one-third of the way with water and bring to the boil over medium heat. Distribute the rice evenly on the bottom of a sieve (see note) that can sit inside the rim of the saucepan without touching the water, making sure the rice is not piled too high in the centre. Place the sieve in the saucepan, cover with a lid and steam for about 20 minutes, or until the rice is tender.

2 Meanwhile, warm the coconut milk, caster sugar and salt in a small saucepan over low heat until the sugar has dissolved, taking care not to let the mixture boil. Remove from the heat. Mix the turmeric with 2–3 tablespoons warm water until smooth, then stir into the sweetened coconut cream.

3 Once the sticky rice is cooked, transfer to a large mixing bowl. Slowly pour the coconut milk mixture over the rice and stir to incorporate, then cover and set aside for 15 minutes to absorb the flavour and colour from the coconut milk. Allow to cool to room temperature.

4 Meanwhile, make the sweetened prawns. In a food processor, blend the white peppercorns, coriander roots and garlic into a paste.

5 Heat the oil in a frying pan over high heat until it shimmers. Add the garlic mixture and stir-fry for 1 minute, until fragrant, then mix in the kaffir lime leaves. Add the minced prawns and stir-fry until almost cooked, then stir through the caster sugar and salt, cooking until the sugar has dissolved. Mix in the shredded coconut; at this stage, the mixture will be quite dry.

6 Add the food colouring, if using, to the coconut cream and mix well to combine. Pour the coconut cream into the sweetened prawn mixture and stir until well incorporated. Remove from the heat and allow to cool to room temperature.

7 To serve, divide the yellow sticky rice among six bowls and top with the sweetened prawn mixture.

Note
Steaming is the best method of cooking sticky rice. A Thai-style sticky-rice steamer, made of tightly woven strips of bamboo, works best, but a Chinese-style bamboo steamer (or a metal one) lined with muslin (cheesecloth) also works well in a pinch, as does the sieve method used in this recipe.

LA

Late

When it comes to its culinary scene, Bangkok never sleeps. As the sun sets, the city lights up with an irresistible night atmosphere that entices tourists and locals alike out onto the streets. Dinner is a big deal for most Thai people: families gather around dining tables, sharing home-cooked meals and conversation; others relax over jugs of beer and a procession of dishes after a hard day at work; while those looking to dine out are faced with endless options. Bangkok is a city of street food, and in our opinion the best way to experience the culinary culture of Thailand is to visit one of the many vendors that dot the city blocks.

A typical Thai dinner might include curries, salads, stir-fries and soups, all served with steamed jasmine rice. Single dishes, such as noodles and fried rice, are also favoured by some; there are no hard and fast rules about what to eat (and when) here. Desserts can vary from simple fruit platters to sago in coconut cream and sweetened glutinous rice. Tea stalls around town offer Thai-style black coffee, milk tea and soft bread served with kaya (coconut jam) or pandan custard until late.

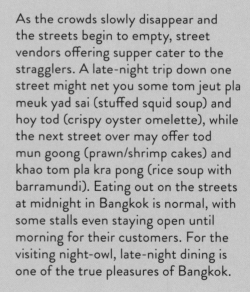

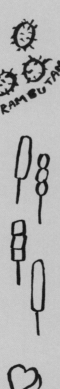

Your options are not limited to Thai food, either. Chinese, Italian, French, Korean and Japanese food are loved by the city's inhabitants. Yaowarat, or Chinatown, is the obvious choice for Chinese restaurants; Sathorn and Sukhumvit are home to Michelin-starred fine-dining destinations serving tasting menus with cocktails and wines or Japanese omakase with sake. If you're still full from the day's eating, Bangkok's many rooftop bars provide perfect spots to take in the sunset and the city view.

As the crowds slowly disappear and the streets begin to empty, street vendors offering supper cater to the stragglers. A late-night trip down one street might net you some tom jeut pla meuk yad sai (stuffed squid soup) and hoy tod (crispy oyster omelette), while the next street over may offer tod mun goong (prawn/shrimp cakes) and khao tom pla kra pong (rice soup with barramundi). Eating out on the streets at midnight in Bangkok is normal, with some stalls even staying open until morning for their customers. For the visiting night-owl, late-night dining is one of the true pleasures of Bangkok.

HOY TOD

Crispy oyster omelette

Hoy tod is one of those special dishes that has a different variation in every region of Thailand. Originally from China, hoy tod has been modified to suit the Thai palate, and generally consists of three main ingredients: flour, eggs and oysters (or mussels). It's considered to be one of the best street foods in Bangkok, where its vendors are easily recognised by their signature huge metal pans sizzling with hot oil. Hoy tod should be eaten fresh, while still hot, as it loses its crispiness once it cools to room temperature.

Serves 2

1 tablespoon rice flour

1 tablespoon tapioca flour

2 tablespoons plain (all-purpose) flour

pinch of fine sea salt

½ teaspoon ground white pepper, plus extra to serve

1 tablespoon baking powder

70 ml (2¼ fl oz) iced water or sparkling water

12 oysters, shucked

80 ml (2½ fl oz/⅓ cup) vegetable oil

1 garlic clove, finely chopped

1 egg, beaten

90 g (3 oz/1 cup) bean sprouts

1 tablespoon soy sauce

coriander (cilantro) leaves and chopped chives, to garnish

Dipping sauce

60 ml (2 fl oz/¼ cup) Sriracha (see glossary)

1 tablespoon caster (superfine) sugar

¼ teaspoon fine sea salt

1 tablespoon white vinegar

1 First, prepare the dipping sauce. Combine the Sriracha, caster sugar, salt, white vinegar and 1 tablespoon water in a small saucepan over medium heat. Stir until the sugar dissolves, remove from the heat and set aside.

2 In a mixing bowl, whisk together the flours, salt, pepper, baking powder and iced water. Add the oysters and mix thoroughly, then set aside.

3 Heat the oil in a wok or a large heavy-based frying pan over medium heat and sauté the garlic until fragrant. Add the oyster batter to the wok, using a spatula to distribute the oysters evenly, and cook for 1 minute, or until the bottom starts to turn a golden colour. Pour the beaten egg over the top, spreading it evenly with a spatula, and continue to cook until the bottom turns golden brown. Flip the omelette and cook for a further 3–5 minutes, until golden brown and crisp. Transfer to a plate and set aside.

4 In the same wok or frying pan, stir-fry the bean sprouts with the soy sauce for 30 seconds. Remove from the heat and arrange in a mound on a serving plate. Place the omelette on top of the bean sprouts, scatter with coriander and chives, season with ground white pepper and serve with the dipping sauce alongside.

Tod mun goong

Prawn cakes

Tod mun pla (fishcakes) and tod mun goong (prawn/shrimp cakes) were originally devised by Thai cooks as a way of preserving food and preventing waste. For fishcakes, fish (and sometimes prawn) meat is mashed until almost a purée, combined with curry paste and snake (yard-long) beans, and then deep-fried. The preparation of prawn cakes is slightly different to that of fishcakes, as the prawn mixture is first coated with panko (Japanese breadcrumbs) before frying, yielding a crispier texture. They are usually accompanied by a sweet plum dipping sauce, but can also be served with Cucumber relish (page 194). Tod mun originated in central Thailand and has always been a part of the cuisine served at locals' dining tables.

Serves 4–6

1 tablespoon whole white peppercorns

2 garlic cloves

2 coriander (cilantro) roots, scraped clean

500 g (1 lb 2 oz) banana prawn (shrimp) meat, finely chopped

120 g (4 oz) pork back fat, finely chopped

2 tablespoons shrimp fat or tomalley (see note)

2 tablespoons oyster sauce

2 tablespoons soy sauce

130 g (4½ oz) plain (all-purpose) flour

1 egg, beaten

120 g (4 oz/2 cups) panko (Japanese breadcrumbs)

1 litre (1 quart/4 cups) vegetable oil, for deep-frying

Cucumber relish (page 194), to serve

Dipping sauce

1 tablespoon whole white peppercorns

1 tablespoon cumin seeds, toasted

5 pickled plums (see glossary), deseeded and finely chopped

3 tablespoons pickled plum juice

250 g (9 oz) caster (superfine) sugar

1 tablespoon fine sea salt

2 tablespoons white vinegar

5 garlic cloves, finely chopped

4 cloves

1 cinnamon stick

2 coriander seeds

1 First, prepare the dipping sauce. Using a mortar and pestle, pound the white peppercorns into a fine powder. Transfer to a saucepan, along with 500 ml (17 fl oz/2 cups) water and the rest of the ingredients, and bring to the boil over medium heat. Reduce the heat to low and simmer for a further 20 minutes, until the pickled plum becomes very soft. Strain through a sieve into an airtight jar and set aside to cool to room temperature in the refrigerator, where it will also keep for 2–3 days.

2 Using a mortar and pestle, pound the white peppercorns into a fine powder, then add the garlic and coriander root and pound into a fine paste. Transfer the paste to a large mixing bowl and add the prawn meat, pork fat, shrimp fat, oyster sauce and soy sauce and mix well to combine. Gather the mixture into a ball and throw it into the bottom of the bowl so that it makes a loud slapping noise. Repeat the slapping process for 5 minutes, until the mixture thickens and becomes sticky.

3 Using wet hands, take a golf ball–sized portion of the mixture and flatten it into a cake 4–5 cm (1½–2 in) in diameter. Place the cake on a tray and repeat with the remaining mixture.

4 Prepare a crumbing station with a bowl of flour, a bowl of beaten egg and the panko spread out on a large plate or tray. Dip the prawn cakes first into the bowl of flour, then into the egg, and finally cover with the panko, pressing lightly on the cakes to make sure the crumbs stick.

5 Heat the oil in a wok or a deep heavy-based frying pan over medium heat until a cube of bread dropped into the oil browns in 30 seconds – approximately 180°C (350°F). Fry the prawn cakes until golden all over and cooked through, then remove from the oil with a slotted spoon and drain on paper towel. Serve hot with the dipping sauce and cucumber relish.

Note

Shrimp fat and tomalley are common ingredients in Thai cooking. Shrimp fat is the creamy paste found in the body cavity of prawns and shrimp, while tomalley is found in lobsters. Shrimp fat can be found in Asian supermarkets and is usually labelled as 'shrimp paste in oil' or 'shrimp fat in oil'. For this recipe, fresh shrimp fat or tomalley is recommended, but the packaged variety will also work.

TOM YUM GOONG MA PRAOW AON

Hot and sour prawn soup with young coconut

Tom yum is one of Thailand's best-known dishes, and immediately comes to mind when one thinks of Thai food. Native to central Thailand, tom yum can now be found everywhere in the country – as well as in every Thai restaurant outside of the country. With its complex blend of herbs and signature salty-sour-spicy flavour, it's the epitome of Thai cuisine – all in one bowl of soup.

There are two types of tom yum: a clear soup, which is the more traditional version, and a thicker soup, a modern take on the dish that adds milk for a creamier flavour. This recipe is for the traditional, clear style of tom yum; it's incredibly simple to make and worth the effort.

Serves 2–4

400 g (14 oz) tiger prawns (shrimp)

1 litre (1 quart/4 cups) Pork stock (page 192), Chicken stock (page 193) or water

1 tablespoon fine sea salt

4–8 red bird's eye chillies, plus extra if necessary

2 lemongrass stalks, roughly chopped

1 whole small galangal root, cut into 5 pieces

4 kaffir lime leaves, torn

2 tablespoons fish sauce, plus extra if necessary

3 tablespoons lime juice, plus extra if necessary

meat of 1 young coconut, torn, to garnish

coriander (cilantro) leaves, to garnish

steamed jasmine rice, to serve

1 Peel and devein the prawns, placing the heads and shells in a colander and setting aside the prawn meat. Rinse the heads and shells under cold running water and set aside.

2 In a large saucepan over medium heat, combine the stock and salt, stirring to dissolve the salt. Add the prawn heads and shells, bring to the boil and simmer for 10–15 minutes, until the red oil from the prawn heads begins to float on the surface. Remove from the heat and strain the liquid through a sieve into another large saucepan, pressing down on the heads and shells to extract as much flavour as possible. Discard the heads and shells.

3 In a mortar and pestle, bruise the chillies, lemongrass and galangal and place in the saucepan, along with the kaffir lime leaves. Return the stock to the heat and bring to the boil.

4 Add the fish sauce and prawns and simmer, uncovered, until the prawns change colour. Quickly remove from the heat and add the lime juice.

5 Check the soup for seasoning; it should have a balance of salty, sour and spicy flavours. Adjust the seasoning with extra fish sauce, lime juice or bruised chillies if necessary.

6 Ladle the soup into bowls and garnish with the young coconut meat and coriander. Serve hot with steamed jasmine rice.

TOM JEUT PLA MEUK YAD SAI

Stuffed squid soup

This soup is a favourite dish of the Thai home cook. Pla meuk, or squid, is stuffed with minced (ground) pork, then served in a mild soup, often with rice or noodles. The texture of the stuffed squid in particular is excellent, with the tender springiness of the squid providing contrast to the soft pork within. In Bangkok, this dish is a common offering of late-night hawker stalls and is often served with a bowl of rice or Rice soup (page 135).

Serves 2

5 garlic cloves, chopped

1 teaspoon whole white peppercorns

2 coriander (cilantro) roots, scraped clean and chopped

6 small squid, cleaned, tentacles removed and reserved

100 g (3½ oz) minced (ground) pork

1½ teaspoons oyster sauce

2 tablespoons soy sauce

500 ml (17 fl oz/2 cups) Pork stock (page 192) or Chicken stock (page 193)

1 teaspoon fine sea salt

½ teaspoon caster (superfine) sugar

½ Chinese celery stalk (see glossary), finely sliced

1 In a mortar and pestle, pound the garlic, peppercorns and coriander root into a fine paste and transfer to a large mixing bowl.

2 Finely chop the tentacles and add to the mixing bowl, along with the pork. Add the oyster sauce and 1 tablespoon of the soy sauce and mix well. Cover and transfer to the refrigerator to marinate for 30 minutes–1 hour.

3 Fill the squid hoods with the pork mixture, packing it in tightly. Cut 2–3 slits across each stuffed squid and set aside.

4 In a large saucepan, bring the stock, salt, caster sugar and 250 ml (8½ fl oz/1 cup) water to the boil over medium heat. Add the stuffed squid and reduce the heat to low. Simmer for 5 minutes, or until the pork stuffing is cooked through.

5 Stir in the remaining soy sauce, add the Chinese celery and remove from the heat. Divide the soup and squid between two bowls and serve immediately.

KHAO TOM PLA KRA PONG

Rice soup with barramundi

Khao tom is similar to Jok (rice porridge, page 30), but is seen as more of a dinner or supper dish, rather than a breakfast one. It is traditionally made by simmering jasmine rice gently in an earthenware pot; while jok is cooked down into a smooth, thick paste, in khao tom the rice retains its shape. It is commonly accompanied by fish and seafood, and the freshness of the ingredients is key, as the soup has a very delicate flavour. A bowl of khao tom is a light and comforting way to finish off the day.

Serves 3

450 ml (15½ fl oz) Pork stock (page 192)

1 small whole barramundi, cleaned, filleted and cut into 3–4 cm (1¼–1½ in) slices, bones reserved

250 g (9 oz) jasmine rice

3 tablespoons grapeseed oil

2 garlic cloves, roughly chopped

1 tablespoon fish sauce

1 teaspoon soy sauce

1 teaspoon freshly ground white pepper

1 tablespoon Tianjin preserved vegetable (see note), roughly chopped

5 g (¼ oz/¼ cup) celery leaves, finely chopped

1 spring onion (scallion), finely sliced

10 g (⅓ oz) young ginger, peeled and julienned

1 In a large saucepan over high heat, bring the pork stock and 350 ml (11¾ fl oz) water to the boil. Add the barramundi bones and boil for 5 minutes, then strain the stock through a fine mesh strainer into a large container. Clean the large saucepan.

2 Rinse the rice once or twice and drain, then add to the clean saucepan along with three-quarters of the stock. Cook over low–medium heat until the rice is tender.

3 Heat the oil in a non-stick frying pan over medium heat and fry the garlic for 4–5 minutes, until golden. Using a slotted spoon, remove the garlic from the oil and set aside.

4 Pan-fry the sliced barramundi in the leftover oil until just cooked through, then add the fish sauce, soy sauce, and white pepper. Add the remaining stock to the pan, along with the Tianjin preserved vegetable, and cook for 2 minutes. Transfer the fish and its cooking liquid to the saucepan of cooked rice and gently stir to combine.

5 Ladle the khao tom into 3 separate bowls and garnish with the reserved fried garlic, celery leaves, spring onion and young ginger.

Note

Tianjin preserved vegetable is a kind of pickled cabbage from the city of Tianjin in China. Jars of Tianjin preserved vegetable can be readily found in Asian supermarkets.

Tom kha gai

Chicken coconut soup

Tom kha is made with similar herbs and spices to Tom yum (page 131), but also contains coconut cream for a richer, creamier broth. Kha, or galangal, is the star of the dish, giving the soup a mild, spicy aroma. While not quite as well known outside of Thailand as tom yum, tom kha is very popular among Thais and also has many international fans.

Serves 2–4

1 lemongrass stalk, sliced

3 small red shallots, peeled

6 red bird's eye chillies, 4 sliced

500 ml (17 fl oz/2 cups) Chicken stock (page 193)

500 ml (17 fl oz/2 cups) coconut cream

pinch of fine sea salt

1 teaspoon grated palm sugar

10 slices young galangal

2 kaffir lime leaves, torn

100 g (3½ oz) straw or small oyster mushrooms

100 g (3½ oz) skinless chicken breast or boneless thigh, sliced

2–3 tablespoons fish sauce

1–2 tablespoons lime juice

30 g (1 oz/1 cup loosely packed) coriander (cilantro) leaves, roughly chopped, plus extra whole leaves to garnish

1 In a mortar and pestle, briefly pound the lemongrass, shallots and the whole chillies to bruise them. Transfer to a saucepan and add the chicken stock and coconut cream. Bring to the boil over medium heat and add the salt, palm sugar, galangal and kaffir lime leaves.

2 Simmer for 2–3 minutes to allow the flavours to develop, then add the mushrooms and sliced chicken. Reduce the heat to low and simmer gently until the chicken is cooked through.

3 Place most of the sliced chilli in a large serving bowl. Add the fish sauce, lime juice and coriander leaves and mix well. Ladle in the soup, stirring to combine, and check for seasoning; the soup should have a balance of salty, sour and spicy flavours. Adjust the seasoning with extra fish sauce and lime juice if necessary.

4 Serve the soup into bowls and garnish with the remaining sliced chilli and some coriander leaves.

Curries

Shaped by the ingredients and cooking techniques introduced by trade and immigration, Thai curries have been developed over countless generations and many centuries. Each region has its own take on curry, with population, climate and landscape affecting the ingredients used in, and thus the flavours of, local dishes. Northern curries are influenced by Burmese cuisine, and have less coconut cream and more dried spices than curries from other parts of Thailand. Southern curries, on the other hand, are heavily influenced by the area's Muslim communities and share characteristics with curries from Malaysia, Indonesia and India, with ingredients such as cardamom, cumin and coconut cream being used. Curries from the northeast share many similarities with those of Laos, and central Thailand also has its own unique takes. With Bangkok attracting Thais from all over the country, locals and visitors alike are lucky enough to be able to find curry varieties from all over Thailand.

The most important component of any good Thai curry is the curry paste. Most pastes use similar herbs and aromatics – galangal, lemongrass, red shallots and garlic are the most common – to produce the curry's signature complex flavours. The paste must be pounded and worked until it has a smooth consistency, as coarse curry pastes make for an undesirable finished dish with a less pleasant texture. Thai cooks use a mortar and pestle to achieve this – not only does a mortar and pestle produce very smooth pastes by crushing instead of chopping ingredients, but the pounding process also extracts more fragrance from herbs and spices, producing pastes superior to those made with a food processor.

Ready-made curry pastes are easy to find in both supermarkets and specialty stores, but the aroma and flavour of a freshly made curry paste are unbeatable. Over the next few pages you will find the recipes for some of our favourite curries, and while making your own pastes can be time-consuming, we do encourage you to give it a try – the results are truly rewarding.

GAENG KHEAW WAN GAI

Green curry with chicken

Gaeng kheaw wan has been an integral part of Thai cuisine since the Ayutthaya period (1351–1767). Originally, Thai curries did not contain coconut cream, but over the generations this has changed, resulting in the coconut cream curries we know and love today. Green curry gets its name – and colour – from the green chillies (and sometimes chilli leaves) in its curry paste base.

Serves 4

500 ml (17 fl oz/2 cups) coconut cream

2 tablespoons Green curry paste (right)

1 tablespoon grated palm sugar (optional)

300 g (10½ oz) boneless, skinless chicken thighs, sliced

1½ tablespoons fish sauce

250 ml (8½ fl oz/1 cup) Chicken stock (page 193) or thin coconut milk

50 g (1¾ oz) pea eggplants (aubergines)

50 g (1¾ oz) Thai or round eggplants (aubergines)

30 g (1 oz/1 cup loosely packed) Thai basil leaves (see glossary)

2 long red chillies, sliced on the diagonal

2 kaffir lime leaves, very finely sliced

steamed jasmine rice, to serve

Green curry paste (see note)

½ teaspoon coriander seeds

¼ teaspoon cumin seeds

½ tablespoon white peppercorns

2 tablespoons chopped green bird's eye chilli

1 teaspoon fine sea salt

3 coriander (cilantro) roots, scraped clean and chopped

1 kaffir lime leaf, very finely chopped

1 × 2 cm (¾ in) piece galangal, chopped

1 lemongrass stalk, finely sliced

1 cm (½ in) piece turmeric, chopped

1½ red shallots, diced

4 garlic cloves, diced

1 teaspoon gapi (fermented shrimp paste; see glossary)

1 First, make the curry paste. In a dry frying pan over low heat, toast the coriander and cumin seeds until fragrant and lightly coloured. Remove from the heat and transfer to a mortar and pestle, along with the white peppercorns. Pound the spices into a powder and set aside in a bowl.

2 Add the chilli and salt to the mortar and pestle and pound into a paste. Add the coriander root, kaffir lime leaf, galangal, lemongrass, turmeric, shallot and garlic, pounding until smooth after each addition. Finally, add the gapi and the toasted spices and pound and stir the mixture until you have a smooth, uniform paste. Set aside.

3 In a wok over medium–high heat, crack the coconut cream by cooking it until the oil separates from the coconut solids. Add the curry paste and palm sugar, if desired, and stir well to combine and prevent the paste from burning.

4 Add the chicken and cook for 1–2 minutes, until the curry paste is fragrant. Season with the fish sauce and stir in the stock. Add both kinds of eggplants, then bring to the boil and reduce the heat to low before cooking, covered, for 4–5 minutes.

5 Add in most of the basil leaves and half of the chilli, reserving the rest for garnish, and stir for 30 seconds. Remove from the heat.

6 Transfer the curry to a serving bowl and garnish with the kaffir lime leaves and the remaining basil and chilli. Serve with steamed jasmine rice.

Note

This recipe will make more paste than you'll need for the curry. Any remaining paste will keep in a jar in the fridge for 2–3 days.

PU PAD PONG GARI

Dry yellow curry with soft-shell crab

Pong gari, or curry powder, is a blend of herbs and spices including garlic, ginger, turmeric, cinnamon, cumin and coriander. Although it is Indian in origin, it's most likely an invention of British colonists trying to recreate actual Indian spice blends such as garam masala back home.

Curry powder gives this dish its signature fragrance, and the subtle spice of the pong gari combined with the sweet–umami flavour of the soft-shell crab makes it one of the most sought-after foods for special occasions. Despite its popularity as a celebratory dish, it can be difficult to find in Bangkok, usually only on the menus of more expensive restaurants, and even then, only when soft-shell crabs are available.

Serves 2

4 live soft-shell crabs

2 eggs, beaten

1 tablespoon soy sauce

1 teaspoon caster (superfine) sugar

1 tablespoon curry powder

2 tablespoons nam prik pao
(Thai chilli paste; see glossary)

150 ml (5 fl oz) evaporated milk

3 tablespoons vegetable oil

4 garlic cloves, finely chopped

½ onion, sliced

2 teaspoons whole white
peppercorns, ground

2 spring onions (scallions), cut into
3 cm (1¼ in) lengths

2 Chinese celery stalks (see
glossary), cut into 4 cm (1½ in)
lengths

2 long red chillies, sliced on
the diagonal

1 Put the crabs to sleep by freezing them for 25–30 minutes. Using kitchen shears, remove the faces of the soft-shell crabs by cutting just behind the eyes and mouth parts. Lift the left edge of each crab's upper shell and remove the beige-coloured gills underneath, then repeat the process on the right side. Turn the crabs over and pull off the abdominal flaps, then split the crabs down the centre with a cleaver or large knife. Clean the crab pieces under running water.

2 Place the crab and 750 ml (25½ fl oz/3 cups) water in a saucepan over medium heat and bring to the boil. Cover with a lid and steam for 20 minutes. Drain the crab pieces in a colander and set aside.

3 Combine the eggs, soy sauce, caster sugar, curry powder, chilli paste and evaporated milk in a bowl and set aside.

4 Heat the oil in a wok over high heat and sauté the garlic until fragrant. Add the crab pieces and onion and stir-fry for 1 minute.

5 Pour in the egg mixture and cook, stirring constantly, for 30 seconds–1 minute, until the egg is just firm. Add the white pepper, spring onion, celery and chilli, then stir-fry for 1–2 minutes, until well combined. Remove from the heat and serve immediately.

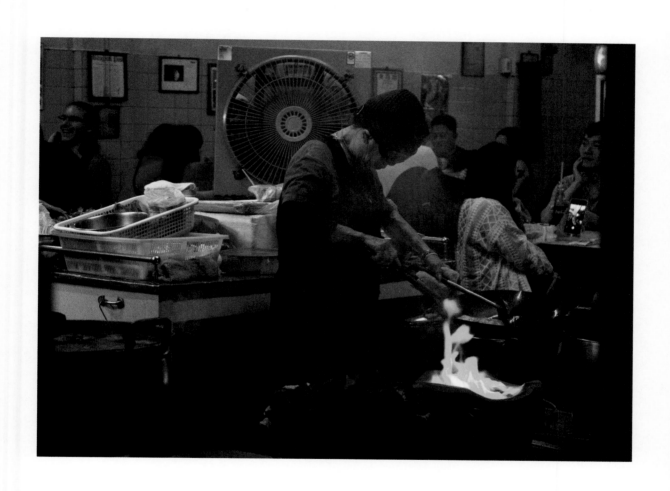

gaeng massaman nue

Massaman curry with beef

Gaeng massaman, while a classic Thai curry, is actually thought to have its roots in Malaysian cuisine – not surprising when you consider that Thailand shares a border with Malaysia and is home to the third-largest population of ethnic Malays in the world.

There are two variations of this special dish. The first comes from the south of Thailand and is common among the region's Muslim communities. It has fewer Thai herbs, is quite dry, and is eaten with bread or roti. The recipe below is an ancient recipe from central Thailand, where the gaeng massaman is cooked with various Thai herbs and finished with a significant amount of curry broth to be enjoyed with rice.

Serves 4–6

250 ml (8½ fl oz/1 cup) vegetable oil, for deep-frying

500 g (1 lb 2 oz) beef brisket or chuck steak, cut into 3–5 cm (1¼–2 in) pieces

4 potatoes, peeled and quartered

9 pickling onions or small red shallots, quartered

5 green cardamom pods

125 ml (4 fl oz/½ cup) coconut milk or water

1 litre (1 quart/4 cups) coconut cream

100 g (3½ oz) roasted peanuts

1 cinnamon stick

3 bay leaves

120 g (4 oz) Massaman curry paste (right)

50 g (1¾ oz) palm sugar, finely grated, plus extra if necessary

3 tablespoons fish sauce, plus extra if necessary

1 tablespoon tamarind concentrate, plus extra if necessary

steamed jasmine rice, to serve

Massaman curry paste (see note)

1 star anise

2 cloves

2 teaspoons coriander seeds

½ teaspoon cumin seeds

½ teaspoon freshly grated nutmeg

2 cm (¾ in) piece cinnamon

2 green cardamom pods

½ teaspoon ground mace

½ teaspoon whole white peppercorns

6 dried red chillies, deseeded, soaked in cold water until soft, then drained

1 tablespoon finely chopped galangal

2½ tablespoons chopped lemongrass

3 coriander (cilantro) roots, scraped clean and finely chopped

4 red shallots, finely chopped

4 garlic cloves, finely chopped

1 teaspoon fine sea salt

2 tablespoons roasted peanuts

1 First, make the curry paste. In a dry frying pan over low heat, working with one spice at a time, toast the star anise, cloves, coriander seeds, cumin seeds, nutmeg, cinnamon, cardamom and mace until fragrant and lightly coloured. Remove from the heat and transfer to a mortar and pestle, along with the white peppercorns. Pound the spices into a fine powder, sift into a bowl and set aside.

2 In a dry wok over medium heat, cook the chillies, galangal, lemongrass and coriander root, stirring constantly, until lightly coloured. Add the shallots and garlic and cook for a further 3–4 minutes, until everything is golden brown and fragrant. Transfer to a mortar and pestle.

3 Pound the chillies, galangal, lemongrass, coriander root, shallot and garlic into a smooth paste. Add the toasted spices and pound and stir until thoroughly combined. Transfer the paste to a small bowl and mix in the salt and peanuts. Set aside.

4 Heat the oil in a wok or a deep heavy-based saucepan over medium heat until a cube of bread dropped into the oil browns in 30 seconds – approximately 180°C (350°F). Deep-fry the beef pieces until golden, then remove from the oil with a slotted spoon and set aside to drain on paper towel. Repeat with the potato and onion.

5 In a dry frying pan over low heat, toast the cardamom until fragrant and lightly coloured. Remove from the heat.

6 Place the beef pieces in a large saucepan, along with the coconut milk or water and half of the coconut cream. Bring to the boil over medium–high heat and add the toasted cardamom pods, peanuts, cinnamon and bay leaves. Reduce the heat to low, cover with a lid and simmer for 1 hour.

7 Meanwhile, in a wok over medium–high heat, crack the remaining coconut cream by cooking it until the oil separates from the coconut solids. Add the curry paste and cook, stirring frequently to prevent the paste from burning, for 10 minutes, until fragrant, oily and sizzling. Add the palm sugar and stir until dissolved and beginning to caramelise. Add the fish sauce and tamarind concentrate, continuing to stir for 2 minutes. Remove from the heat and set aside until the beef has cooked for 1 hour.

8 Stir the curry paste mixture into the beef, reduce the heat to low and simmer for 30 minutes, or until the meat is tender. Add the potato and onion and simmer for a further 30–40 minutes, until the potato is tender. Check the curry for seasoning; it should have a balance of sweet, sour and salty flavours. Adjust the seasoning with extra palm sugar, tamarind concentrate or fish sauce if necessary.

9 Serve hot with steamed jasmine rice.

Note
This recipe will make more paste than you'll need for the curry. Any remaining paste will keep in a jar in the fridge for 2–3 days.

Gaeng daeng ped

Red curry with duck

Gaeng daeng ('red curry') is, as the name suggests, a rich red in appearance. It has become one of the most popular Thai dishes outside of Thailand and is also a locals' favourite. Originally cooked for members of the royal family, red curry with duck has become a regular dish for every Thai family. A variation made with pork and bamboo shoots is more commonly seen in local markets.

Serves 4

750 ml (25½ fl oz/3 cups) coconut cream

750 ml (25½ fl oz/3 cups) coconut milk

75 g (2¾ oz) pineapple, cut into chunks

10 lychees

50 g (1¾ oz) pea eggplants (aubergines)

300 g (10½ oz) roast duck, sliced

2 tablespoons grated palm sugar

100 ml (3½ fl oz) fish sauce

tamarind concentrate, to taste (optional)

4 kaffir lime leaves, torn

2 Thai or round eggplants (aubergines), quartered

75 g (2¾) cherry tomatoes

25 g (1 oz/½ cup) Thai basil leaves (see glossary)

steamed jasmine rice, to serve

Red curry paste

2 star anise

4 Siam cardamom pods

2 tablespoons coriander seeds

1 teaspoon whole white peppercorns

3 pieces dried sand ginger (see glossary)

½ teaspoon freshly grated nutmeg

1 bay leaf

1 teaspoon ground cinnamon

1 teaspoon ground mace

1 tablespoon ground cumin

7 dried red chillies, deseeded, halved, soaked in cold water until soft, then drained

7 bird's eye chillies

1 teaspoon fine sea salt

2 teaspoons finely chopped coriander (cilantro) root

1 tablespoon finely chopped galangal

2 tablespoons finely sliced lemongrass

2 small red shallots, finely chopped

5 garlic cloves, chopped

1 teaspoon gapi (fermented shrimp paste; see glossary)

1 First, make the curry paste. In a dry frying pan over low heat, working with one spice at a time, toast the star anise, cardamom, peppercorns, sand ginger, nutmeg and bay leaf until fragrant and lightly coloured. Remove from the heat and transfer to a mortar and pestle. Pound the spices into a fine powder, sift into a bowl along with the cinnamon, mace and cumin and set aside.

2 Add the dried and fresh chillies and the salt to the mortar and pestle and pound into a paste. Add the coriander root, galangal, lemongrass, shallot and garlic, pounding until smooth after each addition. Finally, add the gapi and the ground spices and pound and stir the mixture until you have a smooth, uniform paste. Set aside.

3 In a wok over medium–high heat, crack the coconut cream by cooking it until the oil separates from the coconut solids. Add the curry paste and cook, stirring frequently to prevent the paste from burning, for 10 minutes, until fragrant, oily and sizzling. Add the coconut milk and bring to the boil; the mixture should be thick and a rich orange-red.

4 Stir in the pineapple, lychee and pea eggplants, reduce the heat to medium and simmer for 2–3 minutes. Add the duck, palm sugar and fish sauce and cook, stirring, until the sugar dissolves.

5 Check the seasoning; if the curry is too sweet from the fruit, add a little tamarind concentrate to taste to balance it out. Add the kaffir lime leaves and simmer for 5 minutes, then add the Thai or round eggplant and cherry tomatoes and allow them to cook until they soften. Stir in the basil leaves, remove from the heat and serve immediately with steamed jasmine rice.

Clockwise from left: Dry yellow curry with soft-shell crab (page 142); Jungle curry with pork (page 154); Red curry with prawn (page 150); Steamed fish curry (page 156); Green curry with chicken (page 140); Massaman curry with beef (page 144).

CHU CHEE GOONG

Red curry with prawn

Chu chee goong is another curry widely popular in Thailand. Here the recipe calls for prawns (shrimp), but fish, especially horse mackerel (one of the important fishes in Thai cuisine), is also common. It's a semi-dry curry, rich and creamy without too much curry sauce, and is perfect accompanied by steamed rice.

Serves 2

250 ml (8½ fl oz/1 cup) vegetable oil

200 g (7 oz) river or king prawns (shrimp), or 1 × 1 kg (2 lb 3 oz) lobster split in half

3 tablespoons Red curry paste (right)

250 ml (8½ fl oz/1 cup) coconut cream

1½ teaspoons grated palm sugar, plus extra if necessary

1 tablespoon fish sauce, plus extra if necessary

2 kaffir lime leaves, very finely sliced

15 g (½ oz/½ cup loosely packed) hoary (lemon) basil leaves (see glossary)

1 long red chilli, deseeded and sliced on the diagonal

1 long green chilli, deseeded and sliced on the diagonal

steamed jasmine rice, to serve

Red curry paste (see note)

6 dried red chillies, deseeded, soaked in cold water until soft, then drained

5 kaffir lime leaves, very finely chopped

1 whole small galangal root, cut into 5 pieces

2 lemongrass stalks, finely sliced

5 small red shallots, finely chopped

5 garlic cloves, finely chopped

2 tablespoons gapi (fermented shrimp paste; see glossary)

1 First, make the curry paste. Place the chillies in a mortar and pestle and pound into a paste. Add the kaffir lime leaf, galangal, lemongrass, shallot and garlic, pounding until smooth after each addition. Finally, add the gapi and pound and stir the mixture until you have a smooth, uniform paste.

2 Heat the oil in a wok or a large frying pan over medium heat. Stir-fry the prawns for 2 minutes, until coloured and just cooked; if using lobster, fry the lobster flesh side down for 2 minutes, then turn and fry until fully coloured and cooked through. Remove from the oil with a slotted spoon and keep warm.

3 Pour off all but 80 ml (2½ fl oz/⅓ cup) of the oil. Fry the curry paste for 5 minutes, until fragrant, stirring constantly to prevent it from burning. Crack the coconut cream by cooking it with the curry paste until the oil separates from the coconut solids, then add the sugar and fish sauce. Simmer the mixture until fragrant, oily and sizzling, adding a little water if it dries out too much.

4 Check the curry for seasoning; it should be salty, spicy, rich and slightly sweet. Adjust the seasoning with extra fish sauce or palm sugar if necessary.

5 Arrange the prawns or lobster on a serving plate and spoon the curry over the top. Garnish with the kaffir lime leaf, basil and chillies. Serve with steamed jasmine rice.

Note

This recipe will make more paste than you'll need for the curry. Any remaining paste will keep in a jar in the fridge for 2–3 days.

GAENG BPA MOO

Jungle curry with pork

Gaeng bpa is one of only a few Thai curries that contain no coconut cream; it owes its signature flavour to the perfume of kaffir lime leaves and hoary (lemon) basil. An ancient curry from central Thailand, it is now easily found throughout the country, with every region having its own take on the dish, varying the herbs and spices used or switching up the protein – the most popular being chicken, pork and snakehead, an important fish in Thai cuisine.

Serves 4

2 tablespoons vegetable oil

3 tablespoons Jungle curry paste (right)

300 g (10½ oz) pork spare ribs

100 ml (3½ fl oz) fish sauce

1.2 litres (1.2 quarts) Pork stock (page 192)

2 teaspoons caster (superfine) sugar

10 Thai or round eggplants (aubergines), cut into sixths and placed in salted water

100 g (3½ oz) pea eggplants (aubergines)

2 long red chillies, sliced on the diagonal, plus extra if necessary

1 tablespoon fresh green peppercorns

1 whole small ginger root, julienned

5 kaffir lime leaves, torn

30 g (1 oz/1 cup loosely packed) hoary (lemon) basil leaves (see glossary)

steamed jasmine rice, to serve

Jungle curry paste (see note)

10 dried red chillies, deseeded, soaked in cold water until soft, then drained

1 teaspoon fine sea salt

1 whole small galangal root, cut into 5 pieces

1 lemongrass stalk, finely chopped

2 small red shallots

5 garlic cloves, chopped

1 teaspoon gapi (fermented shrimp paste; see glossary)

1 First, make the curry paste. Place the chillies and salt in a mortar and pestle and pound into a paste. Add the galangal, lemongrass, shallots and garlic, pounding until smooth after each addition. Finally, add the gapi and pound and stir the mixture until you have a smooth, uniform paste.

2 Heat the oil in a large saucepan over medium heat until it begins to shimmer. Fry the curry paste until golden and fragrant, stirring constantly to prevent it from burning. Add the pork ribs and stir-fry until browned all over and cooked through, then add the fish sauce to deglaze the pan, scraping up anything that has stuck to the bottom.

3 Pour the stock over the pork ribs and bring to the boil, then add the sugar. Drain the Thai eggplants and add them to the saucepan, along with the pea eggplants. Simmer for 3–5 minutes, until the vegetables are tender.

4 Stir through the remaining ingredients except the rice, remove from the heat and check for seasoning; the curry should have a balance of spicy and salty flavours. Adjust the seasoning with extra chillies or fish sauce if necessary.

5 Serve with steamed jasmine rice.

Note

This recipe will make more paste than you'll need for the curry. Any remaining paste will keep in a jar in the fridge for 2–3 days.

HOR MOK PLA

Steamed fish curry

Hor mok is a dish local to northeastern Thailand as well as Laos. In Thailand, it is made by mixing vegetables and meat – fish (pla) being the most popular option – with curry paste, then wrapping the curry mix in banana leaves and grilling or steaming it. Thai cooks take this parcel of curry seriously, with a very specific method of wrapping the banana leaves to create the trademark hor mok package. Although originally from the northeast, hor mok is easy to find all across the country – and, in fact, the best hor mok actually comes from central Thailand, where the dish is common in local markets.

Serves 4

200 g (7 oz) white fish fillet, such as cod, whiting or barramundi

pinch of fine sea salt

1 tablespoon lime juice

80 ml (2½ fl oz/⅓ cup) fish sauce

pinch of grated palm sugar

2 tablespoons rice flour

175 ml (6 fl oz) coconut cream

3 tablespoons Hor mok curry paste (right)

1 egg, beaten

6 kaffir lime leaves, very finely sliced

2 banana leaves (optional)

1 handful hoary (lemon) basil leaves (see glossary)

3 long red chillies, finely sliced

Hor mok curry paste (see note)

5 whole white peppercorns

3 dried red chillies, soaked in cold water until soft, then drained and finely chopped

1 teaspoon fine sea salt

3 coriander (cilantro) roots, scraped clean and finely chopped

5 kaffir lime leaves, finely chopped

3 thin slices galangal, finely chopped

1 lemongrass stalk, finely chopped

2 red shallots, finely chopped

5 garlic cloves, finely chopped

1 First, make the curry paste. In a mortar and pestle, pound the peppercorns into a fine powder. Add the chilli and salt and pound into a paste. Add the coriander root, kaffir lime leaf, galangal, lemongrass, shallot and garlic, pounding until smooth after each addition and stirring well to combine.

2 Fill a non-reactive mixing bowl with water and stir in the salt and lime juice. Add the fish and gently massage to remove any fishy odours. Drain the fish, pat dry with paper towel and slice finely. Rinse out the mixing bowl and add the fish sauce, palm sugar and sliced fish. Stir to coat the fish and set aside.

3 In a separate bowl, stir 1 tablespoon of the rice flour into 125 ml (4 fl oz/½ cup) coconut cream. Add the 3 tablespoons of curry paste a tablespoon at a time, stirring in a clockwise fashion to incorporate, taking care not to allow the mixture to separate. Add the sliced fish and sauce and continue to stir for 2 minutes, until the mixture thickens. Pour in the beaten egg and stir for a further 2 minutes, then add most of the kaffir lime leaves, reserving a few for garnish.

4 If using banana leaves, cut them into 2 circles approximately 12 cm (4¾ in) in diameter and wipe clean with a damp cloth. Layer the circles on top of each other, shiny sides up, ensuring the grain of one circle is perpendicular to the other. Fold a pleat at the top of the two circles and secure it with a toothpick. Rotate the circles 90 degrees and fold another pleat at the top, securing it with a toothpick. Rotate, pleat and secure the circles two more times, so that you have a basket with four corners; alternatively, you can use a heat-proof bowl or ramekin. Line the bottom of the basket or bowl with the basil leaves and pour in the curry mixture.

5 Bring a large saucepan of water to the boil over high heat. Place the basket or bowl of curry in the bottom of a large bamboo steamer, reduce the heat to medium–high and steam for 15 minutes, or until the curry has set.

6 Meanwhile, whisk together the remaining coconut cream and rice flour in a small saucepan over low heat. Cook, stirring continuously, until the coconut cream thickens.

7 To serve, garnish the steamed curry with a dollop of the thickened coconut cream, the sliced red chilli and the reserved kaffir lime leaves.

Note
This recipe will make more paste than you'll need for the curry. Any remaining paste will keep in a jar in the fridge for 2–3 days.

Pad thai goong

Pad thai with prawns

It's impossible to think of Thai food without thinking of pad thai, perhaps the best-known Thai dish in the world. During the Second World War, when the Thai economy was suffering, noodles were promoted by the Thai prime minister as an alternative to rice, which was becoming too expensive for most people to afford. As noodle dishes were considered Chinese food, pad thai – and the special thin, flat rice noodle known as sen chan – was created as a uniquely Thai noodle dish, including traditional ingredients such as dried shrimp, banana blossoms, bean sprouts and lime. Central Thailand, the home of pad thai, still has more hawkers, restaurants and variations available than anywhere else in the country.

Serves 2

50 g (1¾ oz) dried thin, flat rice noodles

80 ml (2½ fl oz/⅓ cup) vegetable oil

300 g (10½ oz) banana prawns (shrimp), peeled and deveined

120 g (4 oz) firm tofu, cut into 2 cm × 1 cm (¾ in × ½ in) pieces

90 g (3 oz/1 cup) bean sprouts

2 duck eggs

25 g (1 oz) garlic chives, cut into 5 cm (2 in) lengths, plus extra to serve

30 g (1 oz) dried shrimp

3 tablespoons chopped pickled turnip

2 lime wedges

Pad thai sauce

3 tablespoons tamarind sauce

35 g (1¼ oz) coconut sugar

2 tablespoons fish sauce

1 Fill a large bowl with cold water and soak the noodles until softened, about 20–30 minutes. Drain in a colander and set aside.

2 To make the pad thai sauce, combine all the ingredients in a non-reactive bowl, mix well and set aside.

3 Heat the oil in a wok over medium–high heat and stir-fry the prawns for 2 minutes, until golden and just cooked. Remove from the oil with a slotted spoon and set aside to drain on paper towel. Add the tofu to the wok and stir-fry until golden, then add the bean sprouts and stir-fry for 2 minutes. Pour in the pad thai sauce, followed by the noodles. Stir vigorously to mix well.

4 Move the noodles to one side of the wok. Crack the eggs into the space created and allow to cook, undisturbed, until half set. Using a spatula or wooden spoon, scramble the eggs together and fry until golden, then incorporate into the noodles. Add the prawns, garlic chives, dried shrimp and pickled turnip and stir for 30 seconds, then remove from the heat.

5 Divide the pad thai between two plates and serve garnished with the lime wedges, banana blossom and whole garlic chives.

GOONG AOB WOON SEN

Steamed prawns with glass noodles

Thailand is home to a large number of Thai–Chinese communities, with more than 10 million Thais – 15 per cent of the population – having some Chinese ancestry. As a result, Chinese food has long been recognised as an important part of Thai cuisine. Goong aob woon sen is a very popular Chinese dish in Thailand, and is usually served in Chinese and seafood restaurants rather than on the streets. Clay pots are typically used for cooking and serving, thanks to their excellent heat-retention properties, but this recipe requires only a wok or a large saucepan.

Serves 2–3

100 g (3½ oz) dried glass noodles

1 tablespoon oyster sauce

2 tablespoons soy sauce

1 tablespoon dark soy sauce

2 teaspoons caster (superfine) sugar

1 teaspoon sesame oil

1 teaspoon ground white pepper

2 tablespoons shaoxing rice wine

1 teaspoon whole black peppercorns

3 tablespoons vegetable oil

100 g (3½ oz) pork belly, cut into 10 slices

1 whole small young ginger root, cut into 5 pieces

200 g (7 oz) tiger prawns (shrimp), cleaned

5 spring onions (scallions), cut into 5 cm (2 in) lengths

2 Chinese celery stalks (see glossary), cut into 5 cm (2 in) lengths

1 Fill a large bowl with cold water and soak the glass noodles until softened. Drain in a colander and set aside.

2 Combine the oyster sauce, soy sauces, caster sugar, sesame oil, white pepper, shaoxing rice wine and 125 ml (4 fl oz/½ cup) water in a mixing bowl. Add the glass noodles and mix thoroughly until evenly coated. Set aside to marinate.

3 In a mortar and pestle, pound the black peppercorns into a fine powder and set aside.

4 Coat the bottom of a wok or a large saucepan with the oil. Evenly layer the pork belly slices along the bottom, then place the ginger slices on top, followed by the prawns. Sprinkle with the pounded black pepper and pour the glass noodles and marinade over the top. Cover with a lid and bring to the boil over medium heat, then reduce the heat to low and steam for 7 minutes.

5 Add the spring onion and celery, cover and cook for a further 2 minutes. Serve immediately in the cooking vessel or transfer to a serving plate.

PLA KAPONG TORD NAM PLA

Deep-fried sea bass

Nam pla, or fish sauce, is one of the essential ingredients of Thai cuisine. Created by fermenting fish and salt, nam pla provides a complex salty–umami flavour to dishes. Deep-fried sea bass served with a tangy, salty and sweet fish-sauce dressing is one of the most traditional fish dishes in Thailand and is a must-have on the menu at local seafood restaurants.

Serves 4

750 ml (25½ fl oz/3 cups) vegetable oil, for deep-frying

1 × 500 g (1 lb 2 oz) sea bass or barramundi, cleaned, scaled and butterflied

1 tablespoon fine sea salt

2 teaspoons melted palm sugar (see Chef's notes, page 10)

2 tablespoons fish sauce

1 tablespoon coriander (cilantro) leaves

Green mango salad

½ sour green mango, julienned

½ red onion or 1 red shallot, finely sliced

2 tablespoons roasted peanuts

1 tablespoon chopped red and green bird's eye chilli

2 tablespoons fish sauce

2 tablespoons lime juice

2 tablespoons melted palm sugar (see Chef's notes, page 10)

1 First, prepare the green mango salad. Combine the mango, red onion, peanuts, chilli, fish sauce, lime juice and palm sugar in a non-reactive mixing bowl. Mix well and set aside.

2 Heat the oil in a wok or a deep heavy-based saucepan over medium heat until a cube of bread dropped into the oil browns in 30 seconds – approximately 180°C (350°F). Sprinkle the sea bass with the salt and deep-fry for 10–15 minutes, until golden brown and crisp. Remove from the oil with a slotted spoon and drain on paper towel, then transfer to a serving plate. Pour out all but 1 tablespoon of the oil from the wok and remove from the heat.

3 In a small bowl, mix the palm sugar with the fish sauce. Return the wok to the heat and add the fish sauce and palm sugar mixture. Cook over medium heat for 1 minute, or until sizzling. Remove from the heat and pour the mixture over the fried fish.

4 Scatter the fish with coriander to garnish and serve accompanied by the green mango salad.

Pad kee mao talay
Drunken stir-fried seafood

Pad kee mao is a very popular stir-fried dish that can be made with noodles, rice or, in this case, seafood. (One modern take on the dish even uses spaghetti instead of the traditional noodles!) Despite the name – 'kee mao' means 'drunken' – there is no alcohol in this recipe; the name actually stems from the dish's origin story of a drunkard who needed some food and had to cook with the ingredients available at the time, resulting in a surprisingly delicious dish – spicy, aromatic and full of herbs. Pad kee mao, when made with noodles, is very similar to Pad see eiw (page 76) – stir-fried rice noodles with sweet soy – but has a different flavour profile.

Serves 2

2 tablespoons vegetable oil

2 red bird's eye chillies, finely chopped

2 garlic cloves, finely chopped

100 g (3½ oz) krachai (fingerroot; see glossary), finely chopped

100 g (3½ oz) squid, cleaned and finely sliced

100 g (3½ oz) banana prawns (shrimp), peeled and deveined

100 g (3½ oz) scallops

50 g (1¾ oz) baby corn

50 g (1¾ oz) pea eggplants (aubergines)

4 teaspoons fish sauce, plus extra if necessary

1 teaspoon caster (superfine) sugar, plus extra if necessary

25 g (1 oz) holy basil leaves (see glossary)

2 long red chillies, deseeded and finely sliced

1 small bunch fresh green peppercorns

1 tablespoon nam prik pao (Thai chilli paste; see glossary)

steamed jasmine rice, to serve

1 Heat the oil in a wok over high heat until it begins to shimmer. Add the red chilli, garlic and krachai and stir-fry until fragrant.

2 Add the squid, prawns and scallops and stir-fry until almost cooked. Stir in the baby corn and pea eggplants, then add the fish sauce, caster sugar, basil, long chilli, green peppercorns and nam prik pao. Stir to combine and remove from the heat.

3 Check for seasoning, adding more fish sauce or sugar if necessary. Serve with steamed jasmine rice.

Pu pad prik thai dum

Crab with black pepper

Crab is perhaps the most treasured seafood in Thailand, and commands a high price. It is often eaten on its own with a spicy dipping sauce, but this dish is another popular option. The most authentic version of pu pad prik thai dum involves stir-frying a whole crab (or crabs), letting diners crack the shell and extract the meat themselves. This dish has pungent flavours of garlic and black pepper, and can be found on the menu in Chinese and seafood restaurants around Bangkok.

Serves 2

1 live mud crab

140 ml (4¾ fl oz/½ cup) vegetable oil

500 ml (17 fl oz/2 cups) Pork stock (page 192) or Chicken stock (page 193)

1 tablespoon oyster sauce

2 tablespoons soy sauce

2 teaspoons fine sea salt

1½ teaspoons caster (superfine) sugar

2 tablespoons shaoxing rice wine

5 garlic cloves, roughly chopped

1 tablespoon whole black peppercorns, pounded

½ long red capsicum (bell pepper), diced

3 coriander (cilantro) roots, scraped clean and roughly chopped

1 Put the crab to sleep by freezing it for 25–30 minutes. Turn the crab upside down and pull back its abdominal flap. Use your hands or a knife to break or cut off the flap and discard. Turn the crab the right way up and place your thumb under the top shell, where the abdominal flap was. Pull the top shell off and discard. Remove the gills, mouthpiece and entrails, then split the crab down the centre with a cleaver or large knife. Separate the claws from the body and crack them with a rolling pin or the back of a cleaver. Clean the crab pieces under running water, removing any entrails that remain.

2 Place the crab and 1 tablespoon of oil in a saucepan over medium heat and cook, stirring, for 2 minutes. Pour in the stock, followed by the oyster sauce, 1 tablespoon of soy sauce, 1 teaspoon of salt, 1 teaspoon of caster sugar and 1 tablespoon of shaoxing rice wine. Bring to the boil, cover with a lid and steam for 20 minutes. Drain the crab pieces in a colander and set aside.

3 Heat the remaining oil in a wok over medium–high heat and sauté the garlic for 3 minutes, or until golden. Remove from the oil with a slotted spoon and set aside to drain on paper towel.

4 Remove all but 1 tablespoon of the oil from the wok and return it to the heat. Sauté the black pepper until fragrant. Add the capsicum and coriander root and stir-fry until fragrant. Season with the remaining soy sauce, salt and caster sugar.

5 Add the crab pieces to the wok and stir-fry to mix well. Add the fried garlic, followed by the remaining shaoxing rice wine to deglaze. Serve immediately.

MOO MA NAO

Pork salad with lime sauce

Thai people love their salads, and there are numerous different recipes cooked around the country, from the mountainous north to the Malay Peninsula in the south. Moo ma nao is one Thai salad that is well known among the local population but not commonly seen outside Thailand. A fresh salad bursting with the flavour of garlic, chilli and lime, it is usually served in restaurants – not in markets or at hawker stalls – with a side of blanched Chinese broccoli (gai lan).

Serves 2

1 garlic bulb, cloves peeled and chopped

6 bird's eye chillies, sliced thinly, plus extra sliced chilli to garnish (optional)

1 teaspoon fine sea salt

80 ml (2½ fl oz/⅓ cup) lime juice

2 tablespoons fish sauce

1 teaspoon caster (superfine) sugar

1 bunch Chinese broccoli (gai lan), trimmed

300 g (10½ oz) pork loin, cut into 5 mm (¼ in) thick slices

1 In a mortar and pestle, pound the garlic and chillies into a coarse paste. Add the salt, lime juice, fish sauce and caster sugar and stir to mix well. Check for seasoning; the mixture should be sour, salty and spicy. Adjust the seasoning with extra lime juice or fish sauce if necessary.

2 Fill a large bowl with iced water and set aside. Bring a saucepan of water to the boil over high heat and blanch the Chinese broccoli for 1 minute, until just tender. Using a slotted spoon, transfer the Chinese broccoli to the iced water to shock, then to a colander to drain.

3 Bring the saucepan of water to a rolling boil again and blanch the sliced pork for 20 seconds, or until just cooked through. Remove from the water using a slotted spoon and set aside to drain.

4 Arrange the Chinese broccoli and pork on a serving plate and spoon the sauce over the top and garnish with sliced chilli, if desired. Serve immediately.

GAI PAD MED MAMUANG

Deep-fried chicken with cashew nuts

Cashew nuts are commonly used in Thai cuisine along with peanuts, and gai pad med mamuang is a very popular use of cashews. Although the dish's history is unclear, there are similarities to Sichuan kung pao chicken, and it's possible that it was introduced to Thailand by Chinese migrants and adjusted to suit local tastes.

Serves 4

250 ml (8½ fl oz/1 cup) vegetable oil, for deep-frying

2 chicken breasts, cut into 5 mm (¼ in) thick slices

150 g (5½ oz/1 cup) plain (all-purpose) flour

6 dried long red chillies

2 tablespoons chopped garlic cloves

115 g (4 oz/¾ cup) roasted cashew nuts

90 g (3 oz/1 cup) button mushrooms, quartered

2 tablespoons julienned ginger

2 spring onions (scallions), cut into 5 cm (2 in) lengths

125 ml (4 fl oz/½ cup) Chicken stock (page 193)

1½ tablespoons nam prik pao (Thai chilli paste; see glossary)

1 tablespoon dark soy sauce

1 tablespoon oyster sauce

1 tablespoon shaoxing rice wine

1½ teaspoons caster (superfine) sugar

steamed jasmine rice, to serve

1 Heat the oil in a wok or a deep heavy-based frying pan over medium heat until a cube of bread dropped into the oil browns in 30 seconds – approximately 180°C (350°F). Dredge the chicken in the flour and fry for 5 minutes, until golden all over but only par-cooked. Remove from the oil with a slotted spoon and set aside to drain on paper towel.

2 Using the same oil, deep-fry the dried chillies until they crisp up and darken, about 1 minute. Remove from the oil with a slotted spoon and set aside to drain on paper towel.

3 Discard all but 3 tablespoons of the oil and return the wok to the heat. Stir-fry the garlic until golden and fragrant, then add the cashew nuts, fried chillies, mushrooms, ginger and spring onion. Stir-fry for 2–3 minutes, pour in the stock to deglaze the pan, then add the remaining ingredients except the rice. Increase the heat to high and stir-fry for a further 2 minutes before adding the chicken and stirring for 15 seconds. Remove from the heat and serve with steamed jasmine rice.

GLUAY BUAT CHEE

Bananas in coconut milk

Gluay buat chee is a traditional Thai dessert whose name literally means 'bananas ordained as nuns' – a reference to the white robes worn by women who have become nuns in the Theravada school of Buddhism. One of the simplest desserts to cook at home, the dish involves simmering sliced bananas in sweetened coconut milk. Usually eaten warm, gluay buat chee has a soft, creamy texture and a salty-sweet flavour, and in our opinion is the best comfort food you can have on a cold winter's night. You can use any type of banana, but lady finger bananas are best for their flavour and fragrance.

Serves 4

500 ml (17 fl oz/2 cups) coconut milk

4 barely ripe lady finger bananas, cut into 2 cm (¾ in) pieces

2 pandan leaves, tied into knots

100 g (3½ oz) caster (superfine) sugar

2 teaspoons fine sea salt

1 In a large saucepan over medium heat, bring the coconut milk to the boil.

2 Add the banana and pandan leaves to the coconut milk, reduce the heat to low and simmer for 4–5 minutes, until tender. Stir in the sugar and salt and cook until the sugar dissolves. Remove from the heat immediately, before the bananas become mushy.

3 Divide the gluay buat chee among four bowls and serve hot.

Khao niaew tu rien

Sweet sticky rice with durian

Glutinous rice is a classic ingredient in Thai desserts and is a favourite for many, especially when paired with creamy coconut milk. Occasionally sweet glutinous rice is eaten on its own, but more often it's enjoyed with fresh tropical fruits such as durian or ripe mango.

Serves 6

300 g (10½ oz) uncooked white glutinous rice, soaked overnight in cold water, or 500 g (1 lb 2 oz) cooked white glutinous rice

200 ml (7 fl oz) coconut milk

100 g (3½ oz) caster (superfine) sugar

2 teaspoons fine sea salt

1 teaspoon white sesame seeds, to serve

4 pieces fresh durian or mango, to serve

1 Fill a saucepan one-third of the way with water and bring to the boil over medium heat. Distribute the rice evenly on the bottom of a sieve (see note) that can sit inside the rim of the saucepan without touching the water, making sure the rice is not piled too high in the centre. Place the sieve in the saucepan, cover with a lid and steam for about 20 minutes, or until the rice is tender.

2 Meanwhile, warm the coconut milk, sugar and salt in a saucepan over low heat, taking care not to allow the coconut milk to boil. Remove from the heat once the sugar has dissolved.

3 Transfer the cooked sticky rice to a large mixing bowl and pour the sweetened coconut milk over the rice. Stir to incorporate, then cover with plastic wrap and set aside for 15 minutes to allow the rice to absorb the coconut milk. Allow to cool to room temperature.

4 To serve, sprinkle the sticky rice with sesame seeds and accompany with fresh durian or mango.

Note

Steaming is the best method of cooking sticky rice. A Thai-style sticky-rice steamer, made of tightly woven strips of bamboo, works best, but a Chinese-style bamboo steamer (or a metal steamer basket) lined with muslin (cheesecloth) also works well in a pinch, as does the sieve method used in this recipe.

NAM PLA WAN MAMUANG DIB

Sweet fish sauce with green mango

Green mango is very popular in Thailand for its crunchy texture and sour flavour. It is traditionally served with nam pla wan, or sweet fish sauce, which has been an accompaniment to green mango for centuries. Nam pla wan is simple to make and adds sweet and savoury dimensions to the fruit. Although traditionally served with green mango, nam pla wan is versatile and complements many different fruits and vegetables.

Serves 5

400 g (14 oz) coconut sugar

2 tablespoons gapi (fermented shrimp paste; see glossary)

3 tablespoons fish sauce

50 g (1¾ oz) dried shrimp

1 small red shallot, finely sliced

1 red chilli, finely chopped (optional)

1 tablespoon chilli flakes (optional)

4 sour green mangoes, sliced, to serve

1 Bring the coconut sugar and 125 ml (4 fl oz/½ cup) of water to the boil in a saucepan over medium heat. Cook, stirring constantly, until the sugar has dissolved, then add the gapi and fish sauce and mix well to combine. Reduce the heat to low and simmer the mixture for 10 minutes, until thickened, then remove from the heat.

2 Stir in the dried shrimp, shallot and fresh and dried chilli, if using. Transfer to a small serving bowl and set aside to cool to room temperature. Once cool, if the nam pla wan is not being used immediately, transfer it to an airtight container and place in the refrigerator, where it will keep for up to 2 weeks.

3 Arrange the green mango on a platter and serve accompanied by the bowl of nam pla wan.

SAKU MA PRAOW AON

Sago and young coconut in coconut cream

Saku is made from the starch of the sago palm, and when cooked its small round pearls are very similar to tapioca pudding. It has been a key ingredient in many Thai desserts since the Ayutthaya period (1351–1767), and is usually paired with coconut cream. Sago pearls come in many different sizes, but the one most commonly seen in Thai desserts is the smallest, which is favoured by the locals for its delicate and chewy texture. If you're unable to find sago pearls, tapioca pearls will do in a pinch.

Serves 4

150 g (5½ oz) small sago pearls

500 ml (17 fl oz/2 cups) coconut water

250 ml (8½ fl oz/1 cup) Perfumed water (page 190)

3 pandan leaves

200 g (7 oz) caster (superfine) sugar

90 g (3 oz) sweet corn kernels

100 g (3½ oz) fresh young coconut meat, shredded

300 ml (10½ fl oz) coconut cream

1 teaspoon plain (all-purpose) flour

½ teaspoon fine sea salt

1 Place the sago pearls in a sieve and rinse under cold running water to remove any excess starch.

2 In a large saucepan over medium heat, bring the coconut water, perfumed water and pandan leaves to the boil. Once the water is at a rolling boil, add the sago, stirring with a spatula to prevent it from clumping together. Cook, stirring occasionally, for 5 minutes, or until the sago is tender. Stir in the sugar, reduce the heat to low and add the corn kernels and shredded coconut meat. Mix well to combine, then remove from the heat and set aside to cool slightly.

3 Meanwhile, warm the coconut cream in a small saucepan over medium heat. Add the flour and salt and whisk until the coconut cream thickens. Remove from the heat.

4 To serve, divide the cooked sago mixture among four bowls and top with 2–3 tablespoons of the coconut cream.

Desserts

Khanom thai, or Thai desserts, are simple to make but difficult to perfect. Each one has a unique name and appearance, with some having symbolic meanings that reference folklore or hint at their origins. Due to their delicate nature and intricate design, certain desserts were initially made only for special religious ceremonies and marriage celebrations, but can be found more widely today.

Desserts from the early days of khanom thai, during the Sukhothai period (1238–1438), consisted of three main ingredients: rice or tapioca flour, palm sugar and coconut. Pandan leaves are often included in desserts from this era, adding a soft green colour and floral aroma. Later, during the Ayutthaya period (1351–1767), foreign influence played an important role in the development of new khanom thai, with Portuguese cuisine having the most significant effect. Egg yolks and white sugar were introduced as dessert ingredients, and coconut cream began to appear in recipes.

Duck eggs are usually used in these confections due to their richer flavour, denser texture and brighter colour compared to chicken eggs. The bright orange of the yolks represents gold and prosperity for the Thais, making them a popular dessert for prestigious ceremonies in the past.

It is thought that khanom thai that contain egg yolks and coconut cream were originally adapted from the famous Portuguese egg custard tarts. Many of these Portuguese-influenced recipes were invented by Maria Guyomar de Pinha, a Thai woman of Japanese-Portuguese-Bengali descent also known as the Queen of Thai Desserts, who held the position of palace cook in the court of King Narai. Regardless of any foreign influence, these desserts are truly unique to Thailand and have a significant place in the history of its cuisine.

While modern Bangkok offers Western desserts such as pastries and cakes, you can still find these creamy egg-yolk delicacies at local markets, unlike some of the more ancient desserts, which have slowly become harder to find. Being able to cook them has brought us so much joy and it is surprising how a few basic ingredients can produce such unique and delicious treats.

MED KHANUN

Jackfruit seeds

Med khanun is one of the many desserts that became popular during the Ayutthaya period (1351–1767), when egg was first used in Thai sweets. Thought to have been influenced by Portuguese desserts, med khanun is made of mung bean or taro paste rolled into balls, dipped in egg yolk and cooked in sugar syrup. The dish's bright orange colour represents gold and prosperity in Thai culture, and med khanun is one of Thailand's 'nine auspicious desserts' (another is Foi tong, page 185) that are served on special occasions, such as weddings and ordainments, to bring good fortune. Even if you're not celebrating an important event, we recommend trying med khanun; rich, creamy and sweet, it's the perfect way to round off a meal.

Try your best to use duck eggs, as their dense, bright orange yolks are better for coating and impart the dessert's signature colour.

Serves 5

560 g (1 lb 4 oz) taro, peeled and diced

250 ml (8½ fl oz/1 cup) Perfumed water (page 190)

375 ml (12½ fl oz/1½ cups) coconut cream

250 g (9 oz) caster (superfine) sugar

10 duck egg yolks

Syrup

400 g (14 oz) caster (superfine) sugar

375 ml (12½ fl oz/1½ cups) Perfumed water (page 190)

1 First, make the syrup. Combine the caster sugar and perfumed water in a heavy-based saucepan over medium heat and bring to the boil. Cook the syrup without stirring until it is slightly reduced and the temperature reaches 104°C (219°F) on a sugar thermometer. To test the consistency of the syrup, dip a teaspoon into the syrup and allow it to cool slightly. Using wet hands, pinch the syrup on the spoon between your thumb and index finger. When you pull your fingers apart, the syrup should form a thread between them. Remove the syrup from the heat and set aside.

2 Bring a large saucepan of water to the boil over high heat. Place the taro in the bottom of a large bamboo steamer and steam the taro for 15 minutes, until soft. Purée the taro and transfer to a large saucepan, along with the perfumed water, coconut cream and sugar. Cook the mixture over low heat, stirring constantly. The purée will become sweeter the longer it cooks; it is ready when the flavour is sweet but not overwhelmingly so, and the texture is firm but not too dry. Set aside to cool.

3 Once cool, using wet hands to prevent the purée from sticking to them, roll the purée into small ovals about 1.5 cm (¾ in) long and 1 cm (½ in) wide, imitating real jackfruit seeds, and set them aside on a tray.

4 Strain the egg yolks through a mesh sieve into a bowl and set aside. Return the syrup to the stovetop and bring it to a gentle simmer over low heat, but do not allow it to boil.

5 Using a toothpick, spear one of the 'jackfruit seeds' and swirl it through the yolk until it is evenly coated. Place it in the simmering syrup for 1 minute to cook the yolk, then remove from the syrup with a slotted spoon and transfer to a serving bowl. Repeat with the remaining 'seeds' and serve at room temperature.

Foi tong

Golden egg yolk threads

Foi tong is a Thai dessert of Portuguese origin, first introduced to the court of King Narai in the seventeenth century by Maria Guyomar de Pinha, a Thai woman of Japanese-Portuguese-Bengali descent also known as the Queen of Thai Desserts. Beaten yolks are passed through a stainless steel funnel with a tiny nozzle and drizzled into boiling sugar syrup in a circular motion, cooking instantly to form delicate yellow threads. Local cooks take pride in their foi tong, both for the technical skill required to make it and for its place in history. Although the dessert calls for just a few ingredients, it takes practice to perfect. Make sure you use fresh duck eggs, as this greatly affects the texture of the yolk threads.

Serves 4

6 very fresh duck egg yolks

375 g (13½ oz) caster (superfine) sugar

26 g (1 oz) fine sea salt

1 Strain the egg yolks through a mesh sieve into a pitcher or a bowl with a pouring lip. Cover with plastic wrap, making sure that the plastic touches the surface of the yolks to prevent a skin from forming. Set aside to rest.

2 Combine the caster sugar, salt and 700 ml (23½ fl oz) water in a large saucepan over high heat and bring to the boil, stirring to dissolve the sugar. Reduce the heat to low and allow the syrup to come to a gentle simmer.

3 Fit a piping bag with a very small round tip (1–2 mm/⅟₃₂–⅟₁₆ in) and place into a funnel. This will help keep the piping bag stable as you pour the yolk into it. Alternatively, you can use a traditional foi tong funnel instead of a piping bag and funnel.

4 Position the funnel over the simmering syrup and fill the piping bag with egg yolk. Stream the yolk into the syrup using a circular motion to create 15 overlapping circles only slightly smaller than the circumference of the saucepan. Rest the funnel in a glass to prevent spillage and allow the yolk strands to simmer in the syrup for 10 seconds.

5 Drag a chopstick or skewer through the syrup to collect the yolk strands, swishing them back and forth several times to prevent the strands from clumping together. Transfer to a plate to cool and repeat with the remaining yolk.

6 Serve the foi tong at room temperature.

BAS

ICS

NaHM POON Sai

Limewater

A traditional ingredient in Thai cuisine, particularly Thai desserts, nahm poon sai makes batters and pastries crisp and keeps fruit firm even after long cooking periods. You can find slaked lime, or calcium hydroxide, in Thai supermarkets.

Makes 1 litre (34 fl oz/4 cups)

1 tablespoon slaked lime
(calcium hydroxide)

1 In a large glass jar, dissolve the slaked lime in 1 litre (34 fl oz/4 cups) water. Leave overnight to allow the slaked lime sediment to settle at the bottom of the jar. The clear limewater is ready for use and can be stored in the refrigerator indefinitely for later use.

NaHM LOI DORK Mai

Perfumed water

Making perfumed water is a simple process, and a pretty one, too. It can be used to impart a delicate floral flavour to desserts such as Sago and young coconut in coconut cream (page 179). If jasmine is not available, other edible aromatic flowers, such as roses, can be substituted.

Makes 1 litre (34 fl oz/4 cups)

1 handful unsprayed, unopened jasmine flowers

1 Fill a bowl with 1 litre (34 fl oz/4 cups) water and scatter the water's surface with jasmine flowers. Cover and leave overnight on the bench until the flowers bloom, infusing the water with jasmine aroma.

NAHM SOUP MHU
Pork stock

Store-bought stock is useful if you're low on time and need a shortcut, but we think that the wonderful flavour imparted by this rich pork stock is worth the extra effort.

Makes 1 litre (1 quart/4 cups)

1 kg (2 lb 3 oz) pork ribs

1 tablespoon whole white peppercorns

2 garlic cloves, bruised with the blade of a knife

4 coriander (cilantro) roots, scraped clean

mixed vegetable offcuts, such as onion roots, Chinese cabbage (wombok) cores, coriander (cilantro) stalks and spring onion (scallion) greens

pinch of fine sea salt

1 Fill a large stockpot with water, bring to the boil over high heat and carefully add the pork ribs. Boil for 2 minutes to clean the ribs, then drain and rinse the pork ribs with cold water.

2 Rinse out the stockpot and add the pork ribs, white peppercorns, garlic, coriander roots, vegetable offcuts and salt, along with enough cold water to cover everything. Bring to the boil over high heat, skimming away any foam and fat that rises to the surface.

3 Reduce the heat to low and simmer uncovered for 3–4 hours, until the stock develops a rich umami flavour with a hint of sweetness from the vegetables.

4 Strain the stock through a mesh sieve into an airtight container and transfer to the refrigerator, where it can be kept for up to 3 days.

NaHM SOuP Gai

Chicken stock

This Thai version of chicken stock elevates the full, savoury flavours of a good homemade stock with aromatics such as ginger, garlic, coriander (cilantro) and spring onion (scallion).

Makes 1 litre (1 quart/4 cups)

1 kg (2 lb 3 oz) chicken carcasses

1 whole medium ginger root, bruised with the blade of a knife

2 garlic cloves, bruised with the blade of a knife

mixed vegetable offcuts, such as onion roots, Chinese cabbage (wombok) cores, coriander (cilantro) stalks and spring onion (scallion) greens

pinch of fine sea salt

1 Fill a large stockpot with water, bring to the boil over high heat and carefully add the chicken carcasses. Boil for 2 minutes, then drain and rinse the carcasses with cold water.

2 Rinse out the stockpot and add the chicken carcasses, ginger, garlic, vegetable offcuts and salt, along with enough cold water to cover everything. Bring to the boil over high heat, skimming away any foam and fat that rises to the surface.

3 Reduce the heat to low and simmer uncovered for 3–4 hours, until the stock develops a rich umami flavour with a hint of sweetness from the vegetables.

4 Strain the stock through a mesh sieve into an airtight container and transfer to the refrigerator, where it can be kept for up to 3 days.

NAHM JIM AJAD

Cucumber relish

Nahm jim ajad is a quick cucumber pickle that brings a cooling, sweet-sour contrast to the Thai table, and is a must-have accompaniment to Prawn cakes (page 128) and Stuffed roti (page 22).

Serves 4 as an accompaniment

3 tablespoons white vinegar

3 tablespoons caster (superfine) sugar

pinch of fine sea salt

½ small cucumber, halved lengthways and finely sliced

2 red shallots, thinly sliced

1 long red chilli, julienned

1 tablespoon unsalted peanuts, coarsely crushed

coriander (cilantro) leaves, to serve

1 In a small saucepan over medium heat, bring the white vinegar, caster sugar, salt and 80 ml (2½ fl oz/⅓ cup) water to the boil. When the sugar is dissolved, remove the saucepan from the heat and add the remaining ingredients. Check for seasoning; the relish should have a balance of sweet and sour flavours. Set aside to cool, then serve sprinkled with coriander leaves.

SAAM-GLER

Three-spice paste

The literal translation of saam-gler is 'three friends' – an accurate description of the harmony between these ingredients, which form the base of many Thai dishes.

Makes 80 ml (2½ oz/⅓ cup)

5 coriander (cilantro) roots, scraped clean and chopped

4 garlic cloves

2 teaspoons whole white peppercorns

1 In a mortar and pestle, pound the coriander roots briefly, then add the garlic and pound the mixture until you have a coarse paste.

2 In a dry frying pan over medium heat, toast the peppercorns until fragrant, then add to the mortar and pestle and pound the mixture into a fine paste. Use the paste immediately or store in an airtight container in the refrigerator for up to 1 week.

PAK DONG ISAN

Northeastern-style spicy pickled vegetables

Also known as som pak, this lightly fermented cabbage from the northeast of Thailand is an excellent side and a must for any pickle enthusiast.

Makes 1 large jar of pickled vegetables

1 kg (2 lb 3 oz) spring onions (scallions), sliced into 5–7 cm (2–2¾ in) lengths

1 white cabbage, cored and quartered

260 g (9¼ oz) fine sea salt

1 egg-sized portion cooked sticky rice

1 teaspoon caster (superfine) sugar

filtered water or water from rinsing raw rice before cooking

5 red chillies, sliced diagonally

1 In a large non-reactive bowl, combine the spring onions, cabbage and half the salt. Using your hands, massage and squeeze the vegetables until they soften and start to release liquid. Rinse the vegetables under running water and drain, then return to the bowl.

2 Add the sticky rice, caster sugar and remaining salt to the vegetables, massaging and squeezing again until thoroughly mixed and more liquid is released.

3 Transfer the vegetables to a sterilised jar and cover with filtered water or rice water. Leave in a cool, dark place to ferment for a minimum of 2 days, then add the chillies to the jar and ferment for another day before serving or transferring to the refrigerator, where the pickles can be kept for 1–2 months.

KHAI JIEW

Crispy omelette

This simple, popular dish can be eaten on its own, with steamed rice as a snack or light meal or as an accompaniment to other dishes, such as Chinese broccoli with crispy pork (page 66).

Serves 1

2 eggs

½ teaspoon ground white pepper

½ tablespoon fish sauce

1 teaspoon soy sauce

60 ml (2 fl oz/¼ cup) vegetable oil

steamed jasmine rice, to serve (optional)

1 In a bowl, beat the eggs with the pepper, fish sauce and soy sauce until combined.

2 Heat the vegetable oil in a wok over high heat until it starts to smoke. Beat the eggs again to incorporate some air, then pour into the wok.

3 Fry the omelette until the underside is golden, approximately 2 minutes, then flip the omelette and fry the other side until golden. Drain off the oil and serve the omelette with steamed jasmine rice, if desired.

Glossary

The following are common ingredients in Thai cooking that can be found in Asian and Thai supermarkets or greengrocers.

BASIL

There are three types of basil used in Thai cooking: holy basil (kaphrao), Thai basil (horapha) and hoary (lemon) basil (maenglak). It's important to distinguish between the three, as they have distinct flavours, and generally cannot be substituted for one another. Holy basil is spicy and peppery, with a flavour somewhere between basil and mint; Thai basil has a stronger aniseed or licorice flavour; while hoary (lemon) basil has a pronounced lemon flavour.

CHINESE CELERY

Also known as leaf celery, Chinese celery has a similar flavour to regular celery, only much stronger. Unlike regular celery, the leaves of Chinese celery are typically used in addition to the stalks.

COCONUT CREAM AND COCONUT MILK

Coconut cream and coconut milk are extracted from the pulped flesh of mature coconuts. They both affect the flavour and texture of dishes differently and generally can't be substituted for one another: coconut cream is thick and rich, while coconut milk has a thin consistency closer to cow's milk. Both are most commonly found in cans, but shelf-stable cartons and powdered formula are also available.

COCONUT SUGAR

Coconut sugar is a type of palm sugar made from the boiled, concentrated and solidified sap of the coconut palm. *See also palm sugar.*

DAYLILY FLOWERS

Also known as golden needles or dried lily buds, the flowers of the daylily are dried for culinary use and added to dishes to impart a delicate earthy and slightly sweet flavour.

DRIED SALTED MACKEREL

To make dried salted mackerel, known in Thailand as pla kem, fillets of mackerel are first cured in salt, then dried. Quality dried salted mackerel is lightly salty, with a deep umami flavour and a pleasant fishy taste.

DRIED SHRIMP

Known as kung haeng in Thai, dried shrimp are shrimp that have been sun-dried, resulting in a concentrated sweet–umami flavour that is essential to many Thai dishes.

DURIAN

Durian is a tropical fruit that is infamous for its strong, pungent smell, which many people find unpleasant. It is large, with a spiky exterior and a soft, golden yellow interior. The creamy flesh has a complex flavour that is both savoury and sweet.

FERMENTED SOYBEAN SAUCE

Also known as tao jeow or yellow bean paste, fermented soybean sauce is made from soybeans that are salted and left to ferment into a thick, brown condiment with a strong salty flavour.

FISH SAUCE

Made from fermented fish and salt, fish sauce is a thin, golden brown sauce. It has a pungent smell, but its flavour is more subtle, being more savoury and umami-rich than fishy.

GALANGAL

A member of the ginger family, galangal has a pungent, slightly spicy and sour flavour that is more subtle than ginger. It can be found fresh in Asian groceries or in the frozen section of Asian supermarkets.

GAPI

An essential ingredient in Thai cooking, gapi is made from fermented shrimp. Gapi is used in various curry pastes, stir-fries and soups to impart a salty, umami-rich flavour, and it is the foundation of the much-loved shrimp paste relish nam prik gapi. It can be found in Asian supermarkets.

GARLIC CHIVES

Garlic chives or Chinese chives are part of the onion and garlic family. A popular ingredient in stir-fries, they are longer and fatter than regular chives and have a distinct garlicky flavour.

GREEN PAPAYA

Red or yellow papaya in its unripe form, green papaya has a very mild flavour and a satisfying crunch. It is commonly used in salads, but can also be cooked.

HOARY (LEMON) BASIL

See basil.

HOLY BASIL

See basil.

KAFFIR LIME LEAVES

Kaffir lime leaves come from the kaffir lime tree, which is native to Southeast Asia and China. They have a unique hourglass shape and a strong citrus aroma, and can be found fresh in Asian groceries or in the frozen section of Asian supermarkets.

KRACHAI

Also known as fingerroot, krachai is a member of the ginger family. It has a spicy, medicinal flavour and can be found fresh in Asian groceries or in the frozen section of Asian supermarkets.

LIMEWATER

Limewater, or nahm poon sai, is an alkaline solution made by mixing slaked lime (calcium hydroxide) with water and, sometimes, turmeric powder. The slaked lime needed to make nahm poon sai can be found in Thai supermarkets.

MAGGI SEASONING

Maggi seasoning is a dark brown, umami-rich seasoning sauce similar to soy sauce, but with a more concentrated and complex flavour.

NAM PRIK PAO

Also known as Thai chilli paste or Thai chilli jam, nam prik pao is a spicy, sweet and slightly pungent condiment made from fried or roasted shallots, garlic and chillies pounded together with shrimp paste, tamarind and palm sugar.

PALM SUGAR

Palm sugar is made from the boiled, concentrated and solidified sap of several varieties of palm trees, including the date palm and the coconut palm. Its colour ranges from light golden brown to a deep, dark brown, and it has a flavour similar to brown sugar and caramel. It comes in brick, cake or syrup form.

PANDAN LEAVES

Pandan leaves come from a palm-like tree known as the pandan or screwpine. They are used widely in Southeast Asian cooking and can be found fresh in Asian groceries or packaged in the refrigerated or frozen sections of Asian supermarkets.

PICKLED MUSTARD GREENS

Pickled mustard greens are made from the leaves of the Chinese mustard plant (gai choi), which are then fermented in brine that sometimes includes chillies or other spices. They have a salty-sour flavour and can be found in jars or vacuum packs in Asian supermarkets.

PICKLED PLUMS

Pickled plums are traditionally made by packing the fruit of the Chinese or flowering plum in salt. Salty and sour, with a hint of sweetness, they can be found in Asian supermarkets, often under the Japanese name for pickled plums, umeboshi.

SAND GINGER

Sand ginger is related to ginger and galangal, and is often used in dishes from Indonesia, where it is known as kencur. It is less commonly used in Thai cooking, and has a peppery, pungent aroma.

SAWTOOTH CORIANDER

Sawtooth coriander is a herb with long, serrated leaves and a flavour similar to regular coriander, only much stronger.

SLAKED LIME

See limewater.

SNAKE (YARD-LONG) BEANS

Snake beans are similar to green beans, except they are extraordinarily long – up to 75 cm (29½ in). They can be eaten raw or cooked.

SOUR GREEN MANGO

The popular fruit in its unripe form, the ideal sour green mango has green skin without a hint of yellow to it and is quite hard to the touch. It can be used in salads and pickles, or, with slightly sweeter varieties, eaten on its own with salt and chilli.

SRIRACHA

Sriracha is one of Thailand's most famous sauces. A hot sauce made from chilli, vinegar, garlic, sugar and salt, it is tangy and moderately spicy.

TAMARIND

Tamarind is the pulp from the fruit of the tamarind tree, which is native to tropical Africa and cultivated all over the world for use in food. It has a tangy, sweet-sour flavour, and can be found in Asian supermarkets in many forms, including pure tamarind pulp, tamarind concentrate, and tamarind sauce.

TARO

Taro is a tropical plant with edible leaves and corms, the latter of which is eaten like a root vegetable in many cuisines. It is very pale purple in colour and has a sweet, nutty taste, and must be cooked before eating. It is readily found in Asian, Pacific Island and African grocery stores.

THAI BASIL

See basil.

TOASTED RICE POWDER

Toasted rice powder, or khao khua, is an essential ingredient in several Thai and Lao dishes, including the famous laap salad of minced meat and herbs. It can be bought ready-made, and can also be made at home by toasting rice in a dry frying pan until golden brown and pounding it into a medium–fine powder in a mortar and pestle.

TODDY PALM PURÉE

Toddy palm purée is made from the fruit of the toddy palm tree, which is native to Southeast Asia. The fibrous flesh is a bright golden yellow, and the jelly-like seeds are also eaten, often in syrup. Toddy palm purée can be found in cans or jars in Asian supermarkets, and is also sold as toddy palm paste.

WATER SPINACH

Also known as pak bung or morning glory vegetable, water spinach is a leafy green vegetable commonly grown in Thailand, Vietnam, Cambodia and Malaysia. It has long, heart-shaped leaves and hollow stems, which have a deliciously crunchy texture.

WOOD EAR FUNGUS

Wood ear fungus, or cloud ear fungus, has a crunchy texture when cooked. It can be found fresh or dehydrated. If dehydrated, the fungus needs to be soaked before use.

About the authors

Sareen and Jean both spent their childhood years in Bangkok, where they developed deep connections with Thai cuisine and the ways that Thais eat and cook. This book combines their love for the history of Thai food and their favourite local dishes, taking you on a ride through Bangkok's unique culinary scene.

Sareen was working in fine art when he discovered his love for baking sourdough and, soon after, for all cooking. Jean makes and loves all desserts, especially those of Thai origin. Most recently, Sareen and Jean ran Nora, a restaurant in Melbourne, Australia, which delivered a contemporary menu with deep roots in Thai food, but seen from a different perspective: looking at the cuisine from far away. They have both just returned to live in Thailand to reimmerse themselves in the country's extraordinary food culture.

Index

204

Published in 2019 by Smith Street Books
Melbourne | Australia
smithstreetbooks.com

ISBN: 978-1-925418-92-7

The moral rights of the authors have been asserted.
CIP data is available from the National Library of Australia.

Publisher: Hannah Koelmeyer
Editor: Rihana Ries
Designer: Evi O Studio
Food photographer: Alana Dimou
Travel photographer: Sareen Rojanametin
Stylist: Nat Turnbull
Proofreader: Lucy Heaver, Tusk studio
Food preparation: Sareen Rojanametin & Jean Thamthanakorn

Printed & bound in China by C&C Offset Printing Co., Ltd.

Book 84
10 9 8 7 6 5 4 3 2 1

BANGKOK
LOCAL